WOMEN
A CREAT

MARJA-LIISA SWANTZ

Women in Development: A Creative Role Denied?

The Case of Tanzania

C. HURST & COMPANY, LONDON
ST. MARTIN'S PRESS, NEW YORK

First published in the United Kingdom by
C. Hurst & Co. (Publishers) Ltd.,
38 King Street, London WC2E 8JT,
and in the United States of America by
St. Martin's Press, Inc.,
175 Fifth Avenue, New York, NY 10010.
All rights reserved.
© Marja-Liisa Swantz, 1985
Printed in Great Britain

ISBNs
Hurst cased: 0-905838-38-6
Hurst paper: 1-85065-007-1

St. Martin's cased: 0-312-88780-9
St. Martin's paper: 0-312-88781-7

Library of Congress Cataloging in Publication Data

Swantz, Marja-Liisa.
   Women in development.

   Bibliography: p.
   Includes index.
   1. Women--Employment--Tanzania. 2. Women--Tanzania--
Social conditions. I. Title.
HD6211.2.S93 1985   331.4'09678   85-2120
ISBN 0-312-88780-9

PREFACE

This book on women in Tanzania has been written in co-operation with the Tanzanian women themselves. It is not possible to begin to mention the names of the many friends with whom I have lived and worked throughout the period of thirty years that I have known some of them, not even of those who during the intensive years of research influenced my personal and family life. Any understanding of women's creative role in their own society I may have gained I owe totally to what I have received from them.

There are, however, some names that cannot be left out. Listed below are the students who did participatory research; for collecting the data on which the individual studies have been based. Except for those doing research in Rufiji, most of the others worked in their own home areas: Cecilia Bangaki, Honorata Bernando, Gladys Chidosa and Alice Nkhoma working in Rufiji; Magdalena Kamugisha and Regina Mutembei in Kagera (Bukoba) Region; Hawa Akarro, Enena Kileo, Bibiana Mallya, Ashiliya Shuma, Catharine Kuwite in Kilimanjaro Region, where Ulla-Stina Henricson and Mary Zalla were also my competent and helpful collaborators; and Hilda Ausi, Deborah Fahy Bryceson, Fatuma Macha and Severa Mlay who did research among the working women in Dar es Salaam. I am especially grateful to Deborah Bryceson who later assisted me in making a study on young children in the Bagamoyo District. This co-operation continued and resulted in her writing the basic part of the chapter on women workers, which she herself has also utilised as the basis for a more elaborate treatment of the subject (*Review of African Political Economy*, 17, 1980).

I also owe a debt of gratitude to Joan Spencer whose skilful assistance made it possible for me to work on several of the individual studies at the same time. In writing the final manuscript and weaving the often very heterogenous material into the form in which it now appears, Jill Grönfors co-operated with me and made this book readable. Aili Tripp assisted in giving the text its final form. I thank both of them.

I further acknowledge the fact that the main part of the separate studies was made while I was a Senior Research Fellow in the Bureau of Resource Assessment and Land Use Planning (BRALUP) at the University of Dar es Salaam under the leadership of Professor Adolfo Mascarenhas. Much of the material has been included in research reports and papers of BRALUP. Later my contact has been with the research section of the Ministry of Culture and Youth of Tanzania. These institutional connections have made me feel part of the Tanzanian scene.

Of the friends with whom I have discussed the work as it was going on over many years and with whose thoughts my thoughts have fused I thank especially Dr Barbro Johansson, M.P., Professor Bengt Sundkler, Professor Marcia Wright and Dr Anja Torssén.

I have been fully dependent on the unending patience of my family: Lloyd, who took over the responsibility for the home and children when I disappeared for weeks at a time into the villages; Aili, who accompanied me on some of my visits to Bunju, Rufiji and Lugoba and even acted as my scribe; and Eva and Lea for their support and love.

There has been an unavoidable delay in getting the final version of this book published. However, this should not affect the value of the material on which the book is based, which in any case provides a longitudinal perspective to the situation of women in Tanzania. Where possible, the statistical information has been updated.

Helsinki, 15 December 1984   MARJA-LIISA SWANTZ

CONTENTS

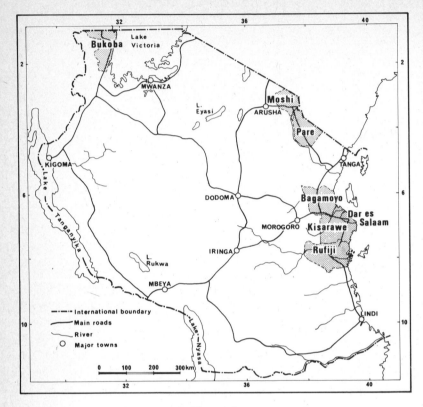

Tanzania

INTRODUCTION

'How could we despise women? How could we despise the mother who bore us?' This was the response of a Tanzanian coastal man when asked about the position of women in Tanzania.

It is often asked whether the position of women in a traditional society was better formerly than it is today. The answers fall two ways. There are those who consider that the woman's position in a pre-colonial society was much better than during the colonial period and even after. Others prefer to insist that the woman in an African society has always had a subordinate position and has been under the authority of men in one way or another. Both these arguments are likely to be over-simplified.

The woman's position cannot be separated from the total cultural, economic and social situation of which it is part. Just as we cannot simply ask 'Was the traditional society better than today's society?', we cannot either ask the question 'Was the position of women in the traditional society better than it is today?' The scales by which we measure today's conditions simply do not apply to the societies of the past.

In the Tanzanian press and at public meetings, women are exhorted to become part of the country's development. In reality it is the women who, in their own persons, integrate the new development with the old. When the newspapers report conferences and seminars held by women or for women, the headlines read 'Women told to produce more', 'Women told to be dynamic', 'Development needs your participation, women told'. At times one sees 'Women told to maintain their dignity' and 'Wives told: Respect your husbands.' Such statements reveal an underlying assumption that, in spite of the workload the women carry, they have remained onlookers who have to be told to participate and to work harder in the process of development. It is assumed that what is lacking is the knowledge and the desire to share dynamically in the process of building a new society. Once the women are lifted from their ignorance, the country will develop. However, there are dangers involved in allowing women to participate in knowledge which liberates. To ward off these dangers the exhortations to work are accompanied by a warning to retain respect towards their husbands. Women must not become too independent.

The woman's position reflects most of the contradictions that are inherent in an African society. The woman becomes the symbol of everything that has traditionally been precious. When the society strives to move forward, sets new goals and, at times, fails to reach

1

them, the blame for any setback then falls on the members of the society who form the link with the past.

Those who desire change fail to appreciate the labour which enables the change to take place. Tanzanian development is based on agriculture, and women form the main agricultural labour force. Not only do they carry forward the traditions that tie them to the forces of reproduction, but they also work the added hours involved in uprooting the weeds that intensified agriculture produces.

When President Nyerere outlined the programme for rural development, he recognised that in the traditional society women carried more than their share of everyday toil in all phases of production (Nyerere, 1968, 339). The women are integrated into the process of development, yet by and large this goes unnoticed. They have not been given due recognition, either, in their role of nurturing the young. What the nation will be tomorrow depends on the work of women today — if child-rearing continues to be the domain of women.

Two essential sectors of national life, therefore — agricultural production and the nurture of children — are in the hands of women, while the men, writing in newspapers, and addressing the women from platforms, urge them to 'take part in development'.

The paradox of the creative role that Tanzanian women play in the process of today's development and the non-recognition of their excessive share in it is the subject of this book.

The research problem, method and data

Does analysis of the position of women in a developing country such as Tanzania require a theory of its own, or is the women's situation so tied to the general plight of peasants and urban workers that the basic theoretical propositions arise from general development theories?

An analysis of the women's position in today's Tanzania cannot ignore the theoretical approaches which recognise how dependent the local economies have been on international market mechanisms, from colonial times up to the present. Market forces have increased the dependency relationships of local economies, but the effects of this development on societies in which people live on the borderlines of subsistence and, at times, of survival, are more drastic than in affluent parts of the world. It can be assumed that the downward pressure becomes intensified in the poorer societies and that women who are pushed to the margins become further victimised. The adequacy of various dependence theories in general and as pertaining to women in particular can, however, be questioned. In view of the fact that a mode of analysis may contribute to further subjection, of people in general or of women, the theoretical approach adopted is crucial. A dependence theory approaches the problems negatively, concentrating on aspects of deprivation of a class of people, but failing to point a way forward. Women have strains and strengths which distinguish them from men, and it is beneficial to them if this is clearly recognised in analysis. When developing a methodology for an analysis of local solutions in social processes, it cannot be assumed that the improvement of the living conditions of peasants and workers in general will suffice for the correction of imbalanced structures in relation to women.

The question which must first be asked is how the woman's central procreative role — which dominates the cultural understanding of life, especially in those sub-societies in Tanzania in which the symbolic view of life has dominated right up to the present, and which the total Tanzanian society recognises as a value — could be positively channelled into new creative roles. If the only way that issues relating to reproduction are dealt with is by the suppression of fertility, it results in open resistance to family planning. Such resistance is widespread. Another important question is what opportunity the women have in their local situations to become conscious of their central role as producers and to improve their own lot accordingly. For this it is necessary to analyse inequalities inherent in the societies of which the women are part, and to examine the effects of nascent or developed social stratification on their situation.

Within dependency relationships, local solutions have a limited effect on the whole. I suggest, however, that if rightly utilised they have the potential of creating awareness, which prepares a way for the correction of existing dependency structures. Activation of the people for their own development is necessary, whatever other political, economic and social measures are taken. Preparatory work on the local level is needed before the participation of the people can become a reality. For this, people's own conceptual and practical skills need to be recognised, and they themselves must play a part in analysing their role in the total development process. This work can become a part of the people's mobilisation for their own development. A variety of natural and human resources are untapped because, outside the communities themselves, there has been little or no knowledge of their existence. This is especially true in relation to women, whose control over local resources has not so far been sufficiently recognised.

Elise Boulding has called such resources a 'power of periphery'

(Boulding, 1977). The utilisation of formerly-hidden powers in the periphery can affect operations at the national level and push for new policies which allow greater scope for local activities. There is a sphere of local action which can be encouraged within a dependent economy. If analysis is made in terms of a dependency which makes the dependent people powerless in the face of market forces, the result is that all responsibility is deterministically removed from the people and they are perceived only as victims of exploitation. This leads to inactivity.

The effects of dependence relationships have varied in different parts of Tanzania. In the Kilimanjaro, Bukoba and Mwanza Regions the economies, which have become dependent on the fluctuating market prices of coffee and cotton, have reacted to the changing situations differently from the areas nearer to the Coast. The latter have to a degree resisted these market forces, after an initial hard experience of forced cotton growing, but at the same time these areas have been deliberately pushed aside as non-productive. Efforts made by the Germans at the turn of the century to graft the coastal economy on to the cotton industry failed. Some cotton growing has continued on the Coast, but its influence on the area cannot be compared with that of coffee in Kilimanjaro and Bukoba Regions, or cotton in Mwanza Region.

In the individual studies on which this volume is based I have assumed that the economies producing mainly subsistence goods and food products are also subsumed, in one way or another, in the circuit of capital and that the transfer from food crop production as a subsistence crop to its production as a commodity has had its effects also in Coastal Region, effects which cannot be under-estimated. I have, however, looked upon the forces of religion and the strength of the traditional cultural practices in this region as counter-forces to the market influences. This mode of resistance towards the market pressures is different from that in the areas more closely tied to the capitalist economy.

The role of culture in development becomes a crucial question in relation to women. Women have continued to uphold the cultural values that were part of the pre-colonial society and which often strengthened during the colonial period. The women's position, however, has been weakened by the way cultural forces have been turned against them. Oppression has been given a cultural dress. Men who have become part of a cash economy have made use of cultural beliefs in order to subject the women who still work within the older cultural framework. For example, men have been able to control the money from coffee crops by asserting that a wife who takes coffee and sells it will not have children, or that if she already has children these will die (see Chapter 3).

Culture must, however, also play a positive role, and must in today's development not be seen only in negative terms. While it is necessary to analyse the ways in which economic forces utilise traditional practices and beliefs, especially in subjecting women to the needs of such forces, the positive potential that the cultural practices still hold must also be recognised. For this reason the societies situated near the Coast, societies which have retained rich cultural forms, are of great importance in the development of the whole nation. Examination of the women's roles there demonstrates that the unrecognised and unacknowledged talents and skills that the women make use of in their daily lives can be lifted to the conscious level not only for the women themselves, but for the people as a whole.

The symbolic dimensions of woman's procreative role are the basis of the socialisation practices inherited from the old societies. Reproduction rather than production is the foundation of social relations, which in turn become the relations of production. The significance of the woman's role as procreator continues to be valued in the present-day Tanzanian society. The continuity which is celebrated at the birth of each new child condemns to futility every effort to discredit the woman in her role as the mother and nurturer of the new generation. The centrality of procreation continues to be reflected in the upheld bonds of kinship and is given symbolic significance in the traditions of respect and honour. The basis of community lies in the total process of reproduction, which includes the reproduction of labour for production. In order to align the analysis with the people's own experience, reproduction is here retained as the germinal category in examining societies which look at production as part of the reproductive cycle.

Power as a theoretical concept, and in its relation to culture, can, in a study of women, be dealt with on two levels. There are two kinds of power struggle in this context. One is the peasants' or workers' struggle for equal opportunities, for recognition in the society. The second is the women's struggle for recognition, for remuneration for their agricultural labour, and in the urban areas not only for equal pay for equal work but for equal chances of job allocation and promotion.

There is no doubt that power based on economic means is a way of subjecting women, especially through their deprivation of the right to hold the title to land. The economic power held by men within a domestic unit is a reality which women hardly anywhere have been able to escape. However, it is obvious that in Tanzania women have utilised cultural means by which they have both risen to positions of social significance and held their male counterparts under their sway, as practitioners of medicine or witchcraft or as holders of authority within the kinship systems. Also, their central role in raising children and in production are cultural means through which women's significance in a society becomes crucial. The question is what means can be used so that these aspects of social life get the recognition they deserve.

Power is always held in relationship to something or somebody. In the context of the wider economy the economic power of even poor male peasants is very limited. However, within their domestic spheres they hold positions of power in relation to women and children. Women's power also has a concrete base in their bodies and in the work that they do. Men are dependent on women for bearing and nurturing offspring, even for the production of cash. This means that within the domestic sphere women have a material base for exercising pressure. The mechanisms for it are not visible to an observer. The respect that a man receives in an African society covers up realities which would make the balance seem quite different if it were understood. Within a domestic sphere individuals do have choices to make, according to their personal ability to exercise the strength they have. In some cultural settings women's possibilities to exercise these powers are greater than in others, and their choices in threatening to separate from or to harm their partner or family are used in different social contexts to different degrees.

The way culture is treated in the study of women is of prime importance. If culture is considered only as a superstructure which reflects the economic base, then the possibilities of cultural means for development are narrowed. If on the other hand culture and the economic aspects of life as a part of it are seen in a dialectical relationship, in which the culture may become a determinant factor in development, then the cultural means in people's possession can be decisive in the process of development at certain periods of their history. Maurice Godelier, for example, uses the concepts 'dominant' and 'determinant' in pointing out that in societies based on kinship relations of production, culture can be treated as a dominant factor (Godelier, 1977, 243).

Culture is not, however, only a means of self-defence or self-affirmation. It is also a people's basic formal expression of the creativity and social communication through which it makes what I call 'space' around itself for its own life. By 'space' I mean the room for manoeuvre which an individual or a group can create by using various mechanisms. Depending on what the resources are, this space is then influential to a greater or lesser degree. Because of the possibility for men and women to create space around themselves, there are also local solutions to people's problems. Even in situations in which the macro-analysis — analysis of the wider society, also in international perspective — reveals an economic dependency, the people in their own experience have social and cultural space which makes it possible for them to become activated and to demand for themselves a larger share of the wider resources of the nation and, ultimately, of humanity. This creates the potential for the activation of counter-forces.

Thus, in seeking solutions to women's problems and asking about the scope that women have to develop themselves, the answers are not only found by solving the theoretical problems relating to the society at large. There is a microcosmic level of experience which allows space for development, and becomes instrumental in further cultural and economic expansion.

In the Coastal societies of Tanzania the women's cultural roles are already recognised within their own system of significance, and this should be taken into consideration by those planning further development in the rural areas. This kind of potential must also be acknowledged in research and taken into consideration as the analysis is made. In a kin society, based on sociality, cultural determinants are pre-eminent and must be recognised as such when the analysis is made. A development strategy which ignores the operational determinants hardly augurs success. An obstinate adherence to a theoretical conceptualisation in fixed categories anticipates results and hinders the use of the existing capacities that people have.

The question of research approach and theoretical formulation is also related to the possibility of finding approaches to development which stem from within people themselves. Here the postulated economic weakness of women correlates with theoretical postulations of underdevelopment and the dependence of developing economies. The same quest for fresh approaches to women's research pertains also to development research in general. The discussion of women's position in developing countries has been a prey to the same logic as the discussion of the development potential of local communities as a whole. It is necessary to probe further into the broader social and economic implications of the less visible and less clearly rewarded work of women and to draw conclusions from it also in relation to the potential power of the periphery over the whole. Within a society which values its communality, expressed in multiple ritual forms, the women's social contribution is not limited to work and rewards from work. Its significance must be recognised also within the ritual social sphere of life.

From the point of view of economic power, it is correct to argue that there is hardly any need to study the traditional roles of women, because it is only at the point of change to a money economy and large-scale marketing that the woman loses her influence in the family economy and in the society. But it is precisely through the discovery and retention of women's social strength and their aware-ness of the capacities they have that it will be possible to turn the trend. It is necessary for the women themselves, for the analysts, the planners and the administrators to build the Tanzanian village societies on the full contribution of women. They can do this only if they all take into account the women's existing — most often hidden — social and labour contributions.

It is my contention that the neglect of the analysis of the so-called 'traditional sector', i.e. the local social and cultural practice, leads to stagnation in the rural development sector, because women's social and labour contributions are not rightly known or estimated in the development plans that are made. Furthermore, the value scale applied continues to be based solely on the concept of eco-nomic power. Participatory research has both facilitated the study of the women's social and cultural and economic roles and in a small way served as a means of making the women conscious of their con-tribution to development. In this kind of research the people's con-ceptualisation of their own social and economic reality and their experience of it play a crucial role.

The participatory research method

The potentialities inherent in local situations, and specifically in the situation of women, can be recognised only if the research methods applied are such that they release the unused resources rather than suppress them. A research approach which facilitates the participa-tion of the people in researching issues of central importance to them is one way of extending their own potential for development. A participatory research approach raises the self-awareness of the subjects of research and assists in creating more space around them for conscious utilisation of their own capabilities. The way we con-ceive the subjects of research is of the utmost importance. The general theoretical framework and research approach used in the studies in this book emphasise the necessity to allow the specific character of the societies concerned to influence the mode of research applied to them, so that the researcher does not become rigidly tied to a set of categories which predetermine the results.

In the village studies, and specifically in relation to women, the inadequacy of survey questionnaires has become evident. When respondents are submitted to inquiries without being given any information on the research background, they may interpret the study as a kind of harassment. Thus biased results are bound to occur. The informants become cautious, and so their responses are inaccurate; they may even deliberately mislead the inquirers. That this is the case has become clear during participation research, when in the initial stages people have tried to use the same techniques which they used with casual observers or with inquirers administering a questionnaire. Only when the confidence of the people has been won through continuing communication between them and the researchers will a change of attitude come about. Then the research results are fundamentally affected, and the information is of a better quality.

Research is almost universally carried out in such a way that its subjects are thought of as targets, even in cases when the philosophical base utilises concepts of participation and action. Traditional action research still formulated its problems from the point of view of the researcher and of science and did not approach the situation from within the framework of the people's own problems. In the individual studies on which this volume is based, carried out by students among women, the first step was to learn to formulate the problems with the people and to perceive the research together with them.

By and large, the approach used was one of participation, whereby the researchers took part in the daily lives of the women. While assisting women in their tasks, the researchers talked with them in their homes and yards, in fields and on paths, at the markets, shops, wells and meeting-places, or on a factory floor, discussing matters related to their everyday experience. Only exceptionally were formal interviews arranged or questionnaires used. Further details of the methods are given in the individual studies. Although the short duration of some of the studies limited prolonged participation, these served as preparation for later research projects which could more extensively develop this particular approach.

The cooperative process itself between the writer, students and numbers of Tanzanian women, was an exploration in search of the creative potentialities of women in the social processes of the past decade, in the light of their mythological and historical past.

The material and contents of this book

The material on which the studies presented in this volume are based was collected over a period of several years, 1972–9, in various parts of Tanzania and in different contexts. The background data on the coastal societies comes from earlier research of mine on Zaramo ritual symbolism (Swantz, 1970). Later, during my appointment as Senior Research Fellow in the Bureau of Resource Assessment and Land Use Planning (BRALUP), I, together with research assistants and female students from various departments of the University of Dar es Salaam, conducted the individual studies on which the main body of this volume is based. Part of the data from the Coast Region was obtained during a research project, Jipemoyo, which was conducted in Bagamoyo District in cooperation with the Ministry of National Culture and Youth of Tanzania and the Academy of Finland. Where data from the latter study relating especially to the Kwere, Doe and Zigua are used, this is separately indicated.

The emphasis is on rural women, although the chapter on women workers illustrates the urban women's dilemma, and a few brief remarks on the role of the educated élite are included at the end of the book. The areas covered are representative in the sense that both traditionally-oriented and more radically changed societies are included, and different geographic areas are contained. The women's road from myth and ritual through the historical development to the present day is presented in the context of coastal societies which have retained many cultural forms from the past. This is followed by a description of the historical development and the present situation in two regions which in general terms are considered to be the most advanced of Tanzanian societies. The urban women represent a further step towards the formation of women as a labour force with an independent economic base. Life stories from a few individual women illustrate the women's path from a creative yet constraining tradition through great perseverance and hardship to a position of new creativity.

The districts and areas represented in individual studies are:
— Kagera Region, formerly Bukoba Region: Bukoba District (Bugabo, Kangabusharo, Kilimelile, Lugaze).
— Kilimanjaro Region: Moshi and Rombo Districts (Kibosho, Kirua Vunjo, Mamba, Mtakuja, Uru).
— Coast Region: Bagamoyo, Kisarawe, Rufiji Districts.
— Dar es Salaam: Ilala and Kinondoni Districts (City; rural area north, especially the village of Bunju).

The samples were small and selective, not random. The material has not been presented as statistical proof of certain prevailing problems, but rather as suggestive of the existing strains and strengths in the lives of women. The proof of their generality became apparent from the researchers' continuing contact with the living conditions rather than from the counted numbers of cases.

Women and ujamaa politics

Women in Tanzania played an active role in the struggle for
freedom when the people's right to rule their own country was
decided. Women as well as men gained — on a limited scale — the
right to vote in the 1959 elections which were to set Tanzania (then
Tanganyika) on the road to independence. Women's support helped
sweep to power the Tanganyika National Union, TANU, under the
leadership of Julius Kambarage Nyerere, and the country became
independent in 1961.

The local administration (Native Authority), which had been
under the rule of the chiefs and tribal councils during the colonial
period, was changed soon after Independence into a democratic
one-party system of government, in which the participation of
people from all levels was considered essential in implementing
development by the people for the people. Gradually a system
evolved whereby the running of the country is effected through the
Party channels, in which the smallest units are ten houses, known as
ten-house cells, each with a cell leader. The cell leaders form the link
in communication between the people and the various Party and
administrative levels — Wards, Divisions, Districts and Regions.
On the mainland there are twenty Regions with four or five Districts
in each.

The first phase of the independent nation's development concentrated on establishing fully indigenous leadership. In one of the first
independent governments, a woman was appointed as a junior
minister. Women organised themselves into a nation–wide union,
UWT (*Umoja wa Wanawake wa Tanzania*), which since then has
been part of the national scene. The first elected chairwoman originated from Rufiji, and had been active in massing women's support
for TANU during the struggle for independence.

After the first organizational phase had been accomplished, the
country could turn its attention to working out the politics of
ujamaa and self-reliance. *Ujamaa*, 'familyhood', is usually trans-
lated into English as 'socialism' and conveys the meaning of the
process of working and living together.[1] Ujamaa policy was spelled
out in the Arusha Declaration in 1967. The meaning of socialist
development for Tanzania was outlined both in action (through the
take-over of the banks, larger industries and some commercial
agencies) and in a clear policy of equality for all, specially articulated in a code of conduct for leaders. Women could expect to claim
thenceforward that Party directives applied to them also. 'A true
socialist state . . . does not have two classes of people: a lower class
consisting of people who work for their living, and an upper class

consisting of those who live on other people's labour' (Arusha Declaration, 1967). In 1971 the TANU Party clarified its definition of development in published guidelines, declaring:

Any action which gives people more power of decision and domination over their own lives is an act of development, even if it does not increase health or food. Any action which decreases the power of decision and domination over their own lives is against development, it retards the people even if it adds to their health and food. For us, significant development is the kind which removes contempt, exploitation . . . and being herded, and which increases our freedom and humanity (*TANU Guidelines*, 1971).

It has been disquieting for many men to discover that these words did not only apply to German or British colonialism, under which the country had suffered consecutively for almost eighty years, but also to male colonialism over the female citizens. The new socialist policies of Tanzania were offering women opportunities which they had never previously had.

The official Party and government policy is intent on carrying through measures which bring greater equality between the sexes. Women's own realisation of their situation, and their intense participation in the struggle for a fuller share in decision-making, will open the way further.

Some improvements have come by means of legislation. After Independence, the first law affecting women was the Amendment to the Affiliation Act, which allowed women to claim the support of the father for children born outside wedlock if the father's identity could be established. The Law of Marriage Act, 1971, was another advance, giving women more security through legal registration of marriages and divorces, minimum age regulation (fifteen for women, eighteen for men), the power to declare the intention at the outset of keeping the marriage either monogamous or potentially polygamous and, in the latter case, the need for the consent of the first wife (wives) to be obtained by the husband before he can take another wife. In March 1975 a further step forward was made by allowing maternity benefits for all women, regardless of their marital status (Maternity Law [Amendment] Act).

In evaluating the women's present situation, we could begin by counting the number of women in high posts. But it is more meaningful to ask whether the new policies improve the rural women's life, and because 87% of the Tanzanian mainland population is rural (1978 Census), particularly how the changes affect the poorer section of peasant women.

The design of the country-wide village development programme aims at reducing women's workload by cutting down the time and labour spent on non-productive activities, such as carrying water, and by offering better health, child care and educational facilities. Legislation was passed in 1975[2] which laid down the rule that all the villages must be regarded, first as cooperative villages and later, after attaining a degree of communal production, as ujamaa villages. All the villagers aged eighteen years and over are members in a registered village. This allows the women to have a full share in village membership, the right to economic benefits, and a share in village leadership. The village has an elected chairperson; a Village Government consisting of twenty-five elected members who choose its executive council, the Village Council; and a general Village Assembly, in which all the villagers have a voice and vote. The Village Government divides itself into several committees, representing work, economy, health, education and other cultural matters. Women can be elected as chairpersons, but at the time of the study only one village had a woman leader. Since then their number has increased. The Village Council had to have women represented, and the delegation sent to District and Regional Party meetings also had to include a woman.

Considering that women form the main agricultural labour force, that over 90% of economically-active women being engaged in agriculture (Egero and Henin, 1973, 150), and that the same percentage of total Tanzanian agriculture is in small-holdings, it is clear that the policies implemented in co-operative and ujamaa villages affect women enormously. The changes taking place in the villages, and their effects on the women's workload and their opportunities for influencing decision-making, are crucial. But this also requires active participation on the part of women to become candidates in elections, beyond the few places allocated to them in various committees on different levels. (The effects of villagization on the women and the new opportunities it has offered are central themes in Chapters 2 and 3.)

On the national scene, special efforts have been made to involve women in public life and to increase their opportunities in employment and education. For example, publicity was given to the first female bus driver in Dar es Salaam, who had earlier been a truck driver on the route to Zambia.

Promises have also been given of greater equality in different sectors of management and government leadership. Women have been trained as agricultural, cooperative and other extension workers, and other occupations previously allotted to men have been opened up to them. For instance, women may be promoted to officer rank in the army and to managerial posts in parastatals,[3] and an increasing number of women have become senior officers in various ministries. Women have been appointed as Party District Secretaries, and since the beginning of 1976 two women have filled ministerial posts and one has become a Regional Party Secretary. Representation in Parliament, however, has moved in the other direction. After the 1965 elections, the number of women in Parliament was seventeen out of a total of 218 Members. After the 1975 elections, the number of women elected from constituencies was only one, but with the regional and national members elected by the House (Parliament) the number came to 13.

In the industrial sector, the Party has at times intervened when a factory has tried to reduce the number of female employees because of the disadvantages to management of maternity leave and consideration for women's health.[4]

When one looks at the position of females in regard to education, however, they still have a long way to go. In the colonial period, female participation in schools was minimal, both because of lack of interest on the part of the rulers in the educational advancement of women, but also because for women the links with the old systems were maintained, while the men were being pulled through trade or employment into the sphere of the white man's rule. However, in the mission schools which provided elementary education in the skills of reading, writing, arithmetic and general knowledge, Christian girls sometimes even exceeded boys, as was recorded in Kilimanjaro area in 1931 (1,879 girls, 1,842 boys). In 1924 the entire absence of government provision for the education of girls was reported, while in mission schools 41 per cent were girls.[5]

When going beyond village primary schools involved having to move away to boarding schools, only a few girls were able to leave home. The number of girls' middle schools was very limited. This meant that only a few selected pupils could reach the girls' secondary school in Tabora, which for the colonial period remained the only girls' school with senior secondary standards.

More opportunities were open for training in teaching. Already at the turn of the century women were being trained in mission schools as teachers, but often they were either former slaves or otherwise less tied to the traditional societies (Anderson-Morshead, 1955, 158; von Sicard, 1970, 138). When girls' middle schools were established after the Second World War, they were boarding schools and the students came from several Provinces. In the 1950s these schools rapidly multiplied, especially the schools of the various churches and missions. After 1950 a teaching certificate required eight years of prior schooling, four in primary and four in middle school. With Independence the level of basic schooling was raised to seven years and the primary schools became coeducational day schools. This improved the chances of basic education for girls, even in regions where their attendance had earlier been minimal.[6]

At the time of writing, women's opportunities beyond basic schooling are still limited. After the seven years of primary education they can go into nurses' or teachers' training, to one of the many government or private secretarial schools, into police or military training and to various domestic science institutes. Until 1976 there was a quota for only a little over a quarter of the total intake of secondary schools to be women. Since then the intake of female students has varied between 32 and 37%. However, the limited scope of the subjects offered in girls' secondary schools restricts their further opportunities to compete for places in order to go on to the senior Forms V and VI after the four junior secondary forms. Girls also become discouraged because of the additional duties they are expected to carry out in their homes, while boys can concentrate on their studies, and because the general atmosphere presses for early marriage. From an early age the girls are subjected to remarks about their growing breasts as a sign of puberty, and especially in the Coastal areas, expectations towards their reaching full maturity carry connotations of its necessary fulfilment in childbirth.

The number of women registered for degree courses in the University of Dar es Salaam has fluctuated from a low 8% to 24.4% (1968) of the total intake.[7] A special concession has been given to female students since 1978 by allowing them to enter university straight from the one year of National Service after secondary school, instead of first serving two years in some place of employment, as is the case with male students. Even so, a great proportion of women students, whether married or unmarried, give birth to children before they finish their higher studies. This is a strain on their studies, and in most cases it means that they can complete their degree only by drawing on the services of some young relative, who is seldom paid more than pocket money and food. For one female student to receive education, many women may have to work with little personal reward. However, older male students may also face difficulties if they have a family to support.

The educational policy of Tanzania was devised to provide equal chances for people from all levels and sectors of society. How fully this can happen is dependent not only on the educational policies, but on the structure of the society and the manner of implementation at every level.

Inequalities are created by the better educational foundation that an educated home provides for a child. It is not an accident that in 1979 more than thirty students from the primary school on the University campus in Dar es Salaam gained high marks in examinations, enabling them to go to secondary school, while many rural primary schools did not manage to produce even one pass. No less accidental are the inequalities in relation to women. As long as there is a great need for labour in many fields, men are considered more advantageous to train than women. Even in cases in which women have chances, there are hidden reasons why they may fail to make use of them.

Many university students in Dar es Salaam shared in making the studies on which this book is based. Their participation in the life of the village women gave us an opportunity not only to learn to communicate across the borders of colour and age but also to understand something of the walls built by education. One of the most significant results of this research was the desire and capacity kindled on all sides to cross borders.

NOTES

1. Since *ujamaa* has become a word used internationally to describe the Tanzanian political line in general, it is not printed in italics after this.
2. Sheria ya kuandikisha vijiji na vijiji vya ujamaa, Dodoma, 1975 (Villages and Ujamaa Villages Act, 1975).
3. 'Parastatal' refers to an organisation which is owned jointly by the government and by private interests, but in which the government has a majority shareholding and determines the lines on which it is run.
4. A case in point was Urafiki Textile Factory (see Chapter 4).
5. Of the non-Christian children attending Leipzig mission schools in the same year, the boys (3,577) far outnumbered the girls (1,874) (Gerber, 1933, Appendix). In 1927, there were 60 government schools with 5,000 children and 2,200 mission schools with 110,000 children (Jones, 1924).
6. For example, in Rufiji in the 1950s there were one or two girls in a class, so that the few who were sent to school by their parents had to leave their homes and go to other areas in order to complete middle school. Information from a woman teacher, Dawa Salum, in Ikwiriri, 1974, MLS.
7. Only half the female students who started in 1968 graduated (MacRae, 1974). In the 1981–2 school year, 24.1% were female students.

1

WOMAN'S ROAD THROUGH HISTORY AND MYTH

Focus on the Coastal Societies

Introduction

The pre-colonial and pre-capitalist cultures represented traditions with adherent value systems which awarded women recognised cultural roles. With mercantilism, the possibility to gain new material goods for consumption, or rarity items as artifacts of pride and prestige, brought about a surge of exchange. The rural communities began to produce both food and utility articles for exchange and acted as primary or secondary providers for the agents of an expanding trade network, which supplied the Western or Eastern markets with labour and raw materials.

With the introduction of the colonial system in the then German East Africa, the barter trade was converted to one of hard cash. The colonial government needed to compensate labourers working on plantations and to build the necessary infrastructure (railways, telecommunications, transport). Labour based on cash wages and imported goods paid for in cash represented modernising innovations from the industrial West which began to change the loyalties of parts of the local communities to interests other than the maintenance of their social group. Men's material interests no longer corresponded with the management of the former material base, which was in the hands of the elders and lineage heads of the subgroups.

There was a shift towards exchange values and hard cash, and yet a sustained effort was made to manage these values within the traditional cultural framework. This development was followed by educational innovation, gradually leading to a scientific conceptualisation of the world by the educated part of the population. This in turn led to attempts to suppress the traditional modes of life in favour of new ways introduced by outsiders. The regions which resisted the Western cultural invasion, often on the grounds of belonging to a different religion, namely Islam, retained more of the traditional cultural forms and a greater cultural coherence, whereas in areas where both the economic and educational penetration was intense, the symbolic expressive aspects of the cultural base gave way to signs of new wealth and learning.

The effects of these changes vary in the way they are reflected in different ecological areas of Tanzania, roughly corresponding to the

17

degree of penetration of Western educational systems and the intensity of export production.

The coastal cultures have been selected in this volume to represent the more traditional modes of culture. This selection should not be taken to imply that the cultural forms which appear to adhere closely to the older traditions are entirely 'authentic', 'original' mores or customs. They too are permeated with external social and economic forces. That which, in the expressed form, seems to have kept its originality has also undergone great changes. However, the symbolic and representational features have often retained their capacity to communicate social values; they convey a system of symbolic communication with role performances. Such a symbolic system operates within a larger framework of a society which is committed to new values and to building a socialist cultural structure on a changing material base.

A study of the cultural scene on the coast can thus help us to discover what changes have taken place in women's situation before the present change in other Tanzanian societies. It gives us the base for understanding some of the contradictions in the woman's traditional pivotal role and her gradual marginalisation.

In this chapter some aspects of the history of Tanzania are traced, as they relate to changes in woman's place and roles, especially in the coastal society. Of the coastal groups the Zaramo, Kwere, Luguru, Doe and Zigua in the present Kisarawe and Bagamoyo Districts and the groups living in the present Rufiji District have been included here. Brief comparative notes are made also concerning other parts of Tanzania. In the analysis, ethnic identity has been retained, although the concept of 'ethnic group' is recognised as being problematic. No static ethnic societies ever existed, and their creation as bordered societies was largely done by the colonial governments, specifically through the Indirect Rule introduced by the British in 1926.

The coastal societies demonstrate that significant cultural features have been perpetuated by women. It may well be asked whether the woman's creative share in the traditional symbolic system could not be more consciously made use of when women's role in social development is promoted today. An important road to women's recognition of their selfhood and their centrality in the total development process could come from this cultural identity, if it were given the significance it deserves. Even in the face of subjection, women have the capacity to respond with resources which are socially enhancing.

The woman's road as charted in history

The period after the middle of the last century was one of considerable disintegration in large parts of Tanganyika. Social institutions had come under great pressure because of the slave trade, which had been utilised in local factional conflicts and had greatly affected women's lives. It was felt most by those of lower status since they were the daughters of junior wives or domestic slaves and were liable to be given as compensation for an incurred debt or as a settlement in a dispute over hunting territory or a slain kinsman.[1] At this period the intensified Islamic influence began to be felt on the coast and inland along the trade routes. It was also the time when Christian missions were being introduced in East Africa.

There are indications that women had not been silent little creatures hidden in enclosed yards and kitchens in the kin and neighbourhood communities before the differentiating influences of the slave trade, mercantilism, intermarriage or subjection by Muslim immigrants and the colonial economy came to be felt. In 1882, a missionary working among eastern tribes close to the coastal societies recounted a humorous incident:

I was much amused the other evening at seeing two women hoeing on the road near our place, when there came past a man with a stick in his hand and a bunch of plantains on his head. The women ordered him to help them carry off the weeds. He declined, when suddenly one of them — a young strong dame — rushed at him to catch him. The fellow ran and the woman tumbled after him. Down tumbled the poor lad and the stout woman tumbled over him. She seized his stick and guarding the bunch of plantains, compelled him to take the hoe and work for her. So the man had to yield to the Amazon and fall to work amid the many jeers from other females.[2]

Historical records tell of prominent women in the coastal society. Some unofficial place-names in the Coast Region refer to significant women who in their own homesteads engaged in business. Women's names had given identity to places in and around Dar es Salaam such as Kwa Binti Madenge in Buguruni and Kwa Binti Lugoma, whose inn became a resting-place for travellers from Bagamoyo to Dar es Salaam.[3]

Most of the eastern and coastal societies were matrilineal when they first came into contact with the patrilineal system of Islam. A German ethnologist Karl Weule, who travelled around southern coastal Tanganyika in the first decade of the twentieth century visiting the matrilineal ethnic societies, gives an interesting account of them. He not only praised the high ethics of the people, but gave a vivid description of a society in which women had a voice.

Here we are still in the matriarchal stage, where the husband is nothing, so to speak, but a connection by marriage. He is his children's father, but is not related to them; in fact he belongs to a different clan.

Weule went on to describe the marital system:

Their marriage, moreover, brings an additional faithful and unpaid worker into the household. For this is the land, where the man . . . leaves his father and mother and either moves directly into the house of his wife's parents or builds his own close beside it. In any case, for some years, until his own family circumstances necessitate a different arrangement, he devotes all his powers to keeping his mother-in-law's establishment. He sees to the planting of the crops and their in-gathering, he breaks up new ground, in short he renders every possible service, and anticipates her every wish.

The impression [is gained] that not only is the relation between mother and son-in-law nothing short of ideal, but that the behaviour of young people to their elders in general deserves to be called exemplary.[4]

Weule was obviously under the influence of the theoretical school promoted by Johann J. Bachhofen among others and later picked up by Friedrick Engels, on the origin of the mother right and a matriarchal system in the evolutionary scheme — a theory which today has got its new defenders among the feminist scholars.[5] Although there is insufficient evidence to support such an evolutionary perspective, the women's usufruct rights to land and their influence within their kin group provided women in matrilineal systems with a more secure social position than they had in patrilineal societies, as will become evident later. Evidence of this is also provided by further observations of Weule, who claims that among the Makua and Makonde, mothers and mothers' brothers conducted the negotiations in matters of marriage and also in matters relating to the choice of the headman. The same practice was recorded by R. Young and H. Fosbrooke in describing the system of the Luguru, close kin of the Zaramo. According to them the women played a dominant part in the selection of the lineage head. In one system, the decision rested entirely with a body of respected adult women of the lineage, and in another the leading men of the group first proposed a name to the assembled lineage women; if the name was accepted, the women expressed it with ululation but if silence greeted the nomination, then the men had to put another name forward.[6]

Under mercantilism, in societies in which the rule gradually became centralised, some upcountry chiefs, but also a few coastal ones, usurped power and utilised it by subjecting others to make tributes. They used the supplies they gathered by means of these tributes and even from their subjects as a means of trade exchange.[7]

In the coastal groups the lineage heads exercised local authority, but only in exceptional cases had they acquired wider territorial power. According to some Zaramo elders who were lineage heads, mothers' brothers heartlessly traded their sisters' children during this period. The matrilineal system, in which the mother's brother had control over the children of his sister, seems to have been particularly liable to abuse. The mother's brother was less personally linked to the children than if he had been their father, and could therefore dispose of them if it became profitable to do so. Thus it was not so much the headmen or chiefs who had power over their subjects; any *kolo*, mother's brother, could become a slave trader when the opportunity presented itself.[8]

Of the ethnic groups in the Bagamoyo district, the Zigua and the Zaramo in particular had the reputation of having engaged in slave trading; they bought slaves and exchanged them for commodities, which they could use for further exchange.[9] In the slave trade women and young boys fetched a higher price than men, since women were the re-producers and producers and young boys were potential labourers. The matrilineal Zaramo also kept domestic slaves until the official decree on domestic slavery in 1905,[10] whereby all children born were to be free. In any case, only the wealthier members of the society had been in a position which allowed them to have domestic slaves. Both male and female slaves were kept principally as domestic workers.

The Kwere, close neighbours of the Zaramo, on the other hand, take pride in relating that they neither kept domestic slaves nor engaged in slave trading.[11] Travellers described the Kwere as fearful, retiring, and living in palisaded villages. This may have been due to their less exposed location and because they were a smaller more closely knit social group, whereas the contact of the Zaramo and the Zigua with the coast was of long standing.[12]

Information varies on slavery among the Doe, who also live in the hinterland of Bagamoyo. The accounts of the first missionaries in the 1880s mention the absence of slaves, whereas an account in 1889 says that slaves were the means whereby they paid bridewealth. The latter may have been a prerogative only of the chief's domain and related to the tribute system.[13] One of the consequences of the slave trade on women was the practice of hiding young girls for fear that they would be stolen from their homes if they were seen, and it is quite possible that the continuing practice of secluding young girls at puberty became stricter and the period of isolation longer because of this danger. Some kind of fear is still reflected even in the Tanzanian government's census figures on the coast which at times show lower numbers of young girls than boys, presumably because the secluded girls are not counted.[14] This was the case in the 1967 census and again in 1977 in several villages in the West Bagamoyo District.[15]

The introduction of colonial power on to the scene spelled further changes. Towards the end of the nineteenth century in the midst of the coastal towns and villages, Dar es Salaam grew as the capital and commercial centre of the colonial state, and rather than serving the economic interests of its surrounding areas, it became a link to the overseas administrative and commercial centres within the colonial economy.

The colonial history of various societies in Tanzania tells of two different reactions towards the invading economic and social forces. One was to adopt the ways of the colonial invader and benefit from the innovations; the other was to resist inclusion in the market economy, with its intensified commodity production and consumption of imported goods. The local societies strengthened their identity through ethnicity, while at the same time employment and religion brought them into contact with other groups beyond their former cultural and kinship ties. The changes affected men and women very differently. It is difficult to say what would have happened if export trade had not started, but one thing is sure: nothing has been more detrimental to the women's position than the fact that men became part of the money economy while the women remained in the traditional sector. In this, the areas of the country that were drawn into the market economy were affected the most.

The advantages that the traditional societies had given to women were indeed, counteracted by the incoming foreign influences. The effects of these influences on men were also full of contradictions. The German colonial authorities introduced the system of levying taxes. First there was the hut tax in 1898 which meant that men had to go out in search of work or be recruited for work.[16] Another way of earning the tax money was to grow cash crops. The colonialists aimed at modernisation — otherwise they would not have been able to create the labour force necessary to extract the raw materials they needed. Men were employed in digging roads, building railways, and working on plantations or in harbours, or as domestic servants in Western or Asian households. Women were largely excluded from employment, yet in many parts of the countryside, the consequence of all this was more work for women since there were fewer workers at home. Women also spent more time on cash crops at the expense of food crops, but at the same time they continued in the traditional sector, with traditional norms, working for family subsistence. The colonial economy was largely built on women's free labour, because it enabled families to subsist on men's inadequate wages supplemented by the women's income. The introduction of a cash economy gave men an instrument of power over women who were not familiar in the same way with the use and the value of money. This together with the educational advantages given to men reduced the women's possibilities of making use of the modern innovations.

Rufiji history as a case-study

The Rufiji river basin forms an ecological zone with characteristics of its own. Its people were considered by the up-country people to be true traditionalists while the Rufiji thought the inland peoples uncivilised. This reflects the pre-Western concept of civilisation as a process of becoming Arab-like; this too is the meaning of the Swahili word *ustaarabu*, which earlier was in use to mean civilisation. The river basin is known as the most solidly Muslim area of Tanzania.

Rufiji is one of the largest rivers of the African continent. It brings its fertile silt from the far reaches of inland plateaux and mountains and deposits it in the flood plains of the coast. A variety of ethnic groups have 'followed the river', as they themselves describe their coming to the valley when questioned about the reasons for settling there. The Matumbi have descended from the hills of that name south of the river, and the Mwera have followed the coastline also from south. The clan-groups from the hills north of the river, who identified themselves as Ndengereko, became the largest single group in the valley, but they, together with most other inhabitants of the area, now simply call themselves the Rufiji. Before the last century the Hehe literally followed the river down from the area around one of its upper branches, Great Ruaha. They intermarried with immigrants of Arab stock and form the present Nyagatwa population at the mouth of the river. Other Rufiji count their origins among the Pogoro, the Zaramo, the Ngindo, the Makua and, as later immigrants, the Makonde. The total valley population is close to 100,000.

The Rufiji have had one main reason for living in the valley, the river itself. In the valley they have produced rice of a quality that no other part of Tanzania can match. The mangroves of the delta and the mighty trees in the forests south of the river have provided building materials for the coastal cities and even for export. The sea has facilitated the transport of these materials as well as the export of surplus food crops to areas along the coast and to the islands. The populations of elephant, rhinoceros and hippopotamus in the vicinity have added to the wealth in the form of ivory and hides. The recession of the waters after the floods leaves the land suitable for cotton growth.

At the end of the nineteenth century, the colonial investors brought in cotton gins and forced schemes of cotton growth on the local population. This sowed seeds of discord and strife which broke out in the Maji Maji uprising in 1905. The whole of southern Tanzania eventually became part of a violent rebellion, which the German colonial rulers ruthlessly suppressed. The rebellion was begun by people in the Matumbi hills who descended to the Rufiji valley — whom those with *dini* (Islamic religion) considered *shenzi* (pagans). This rather recent 'pagan' origin on the one hand and the slave origin of another part of the population on the other hand are still reflected in the structure of Rufiji society and consequently in the position of women within it. The mixing of population from varying backgrounds in the Rufiji valley has meant that social differences underlie the historical development of the area. The prestige of a man or a woman within the local value system has depended on ability, *kunasibu*, to trace one's descent, and in so doing to give evidence that one is not of slave origin. The *waungwana*, the highest in the ladder, claim descent originating from Arabia or Shiraz.

Thus, ethnic, religious and language differences stratified the coastal societies, in which the religious leaders, wealthy traders and property–owners formed the upper class. They had the Islamic religion and the Swahili language in common and could claim some relation to non-African immigrants. However, Swahili was used as the trade language, and some knowledge of Arabic was necessary for recognition as part of the upper class. By the beginning of the twentieth century, the Swahili language and Islamic religion had become predominant in the Rufiji area. The social customs within the religious system of socialisation and social conduct that were developed within the upper class were passed on to the society as a whole and to the lower social groups. At the same time, traditional institutions of female initiation continued in accordance with a mixture of tribal customs, while circumcision was incorporated into the male rites.

The social pattern of the religious élites strongly affected the conduct of all the men, but it changed the women's position even more profoundly, transforming the matrilineal practice of the southern ethnic cultures to a patrilineal or bilineal one. The Rufiji now count their descent from the side of the father, not the mother. The original open yards became enclosed, symbolising the way in which women became entangled in a web of rules legitimised by the Holy Book. The black *buibui* cloth, which first veiled in public only the women of the wealthy 'nobility', gradually became the mark of estate for the upcoming peasant who bestowed it on his women. However, it never became a veil worn over the face among the latter group, for whom it serves as the women's garb when they appear outside their home surroundings; nor did Islam uproot the social rituals of women among the peasants.

In Rufiji, resistance toward Western (Christian) education led the coastal masters to send their slaves' children rather than their own sons to schools; for men education thus became a levelling instrument. But for several decades coastal women were excluded from educational institutions in the Islamic areas, apart from the small Christian fraction of the population.

In spite of having been strongly affected by the colonial intervention, the coastal hinterland had reacted against the so-called modernising influences of colonialism. The coastal societies resisted
growing cash crops such as cotton for export; they were the first to be
exposed to Western-type education, but they largely rejected it, and
they did not allow the availability of manufactured goods to replace
their local artefacts. In 1975, only 150 km from the main city of Dar es
Salaam not only village-made hoes were common but even digging
sticks were in a few places found to be still in use in cultivation. Clay
pots were the main vessels for carrying water and for cooking in
Msoga division of the Bagamoyo District and traditional rituals
formed the central focus of social life in the beginning of the 1970s.
One would have expected a quick invasion of imported commodities
to an area so close to the main commercial centres, Bagamoyo and
Dar es Salaam. Instead, both sexes continued to adhere to cultural
and social values expressed in ritual and material forms. Women continued to occupy a central place in significant cultural roles within the
traditional system, and held positions of social leadership and public
eminence despite the economic suppressions of the coastal peasant
society and its effects on women.

The woman in myth, symbol and ritual

The coastal societies have preserved within their social rituals a
mythological conceptualisation of the central significance of the
woman in reproduction and production.[17] They afford women
important social roles within the framework of their inherited symbolic system. Although the historical process within the coastal
societies is different from that of inland societies, nevertheless,
today's coastal societies also reflect important aspects of what the
process of cultural transformation has been in those parts which have
gone through a more radical change.

The birth of a human being from the body of a woman, paralleled
with the myriad of births from the womb of the earth, formed the
starting-point for female myth in Tanzanian cultures, as it has done
universally.[18] In Western culture the Renaissance still lauded the regenerative powers of the human body, but the rationalism and
scientism of later centuries replaced this with the faculties of intel-
lect, reason and rationality. The difficulty of rationally containing
the wholeness of life has throughout history had the effect of narrowing the woman's role to its reproductive dimensions within the
domestic sphere.

Among the Tanzanian coastal societies the cultural presentation of
the proto-woman as the symbol of life and its generation and

sustenance, whose secrets are passed on to descending generations, has continued within the context of social rituals until this day, but it has failed to capture the imagination of most educated men and women. It could be assumed that as the conception of the meaning of life has changed, at least the poetic beauty of these rituals as central symbols might survive if their significance were grasped in the process of cultural transformation. But instead, under pressure from those who want to replace their own cultural origins with those of Western culture, the symbolic concept of the body is being turned to that of flesh and blood; poetry is converted to vulgar prose, and the woman assessed by her body's value in cash. In other words, woman's reproductive roles are exploited within the cash economy and given monetary value in bridewealth, while at the same time the cultural values of the traditional symbolic system get pushed aside.

Yet there is a persistence of cultural forms which, within the peasant strata as well as among the city-workers linked with their rural origins, often take precedence in their consumption patterns, also within the money economy. Considerable sums of money are spent for ritual purposes. Still today the girls and boys of the coastal hinterland, and even in the city, are taught the symbolic conceptualisation of life. So the proto-women Nyalutanga and Nyapingu play a role in the Zaramo socialisation rituals, which are perpetuated — albeit in abridged forms. Nyalutanga was a mythological creature, said to be the mother of all the people of the world. She symbolised the reproductive lifeforce contained in the female body.

This vagina is large, it has filled the whole earth with people; Nyalutanga gave birth to the whole earth. This vagina has spawned recklessly. This sounds like abuse, but of her we must sing to let the *mwali* [young girl] know that the earth has come from Nyalutanga; that Nyalutanga found out all about foods, to feed the children, it all has come from Lutanga. Then she gave birth to Nyapingu. Nyapingu and Nyalutanga are a person and her mother. Nyapingu went to the men to circumcise them, and Nyalutanga spread it [the knowledge of how to sustain life] for all the women.[19]

It was the mythical woman who gave the people plants and explained their use as food. The myths tell the growing boys and girls that the origin of the agricultural use of plants was with women.[20] The women practised agriculture, while the men went on expeditions to hunt big game. Much of the settlement of the coastal hinterland took place through hunting expeditions, as related in the historical traditions of several ethnic groups.[21] This meant that the daily sustenance of life was left to the women. The men occasionally provided meat and traded with the passing caravans, offering ivory and the women's surplus crops in return for cloth, beads and iron or manufactured tools.

The originally matrilineal ethnic groups have generally retained the ritual initiation of their young people into adulthood. In them the woman's centrality in the symbolic view of life has also been preserved. The influence of Islam has not been able to erase the strong female impact on the conceptualisation of life in the matrilineal ethnic groups of eastern Tanzania,[22] although this fact is not in keeping with the gradual take-over by men of the public performance of social and economic duties within the new political structures.

Through ritual practices, new generations are still introduced to the symbols of the society, and the continuity of the kinship bond is secured. Among the Zaramo, the world around them and their society as a part of it are viewed through the bodily existence of the human being. The presence of death and the forces of disintegration are recognised as well as the forces of regeneration. The woman's womb is likened to a place of death through which the birth takes place. The man's semen and the woman's menstrual blood are the constituent substances of the child they conceive. White, red and black are the basic symbolic colours, drawn from the human organism, by which sexual as well as the moral, social and organisational concerns of the society are expressed. In this framework of conceptualisation, the different sectors of life form a unified whole.

In the ritual instruction communicated to the coastal young people, the female symbolism is central. A human organism remains the same amidst change, and thus provides a constant element in the broader transitional society. It forms a base for continuing symbolic communication which is understood by all those sharing the circumstances and the same mode of perception, even across ethnic cultural borders. In a system projected in organic symbols, all children, male and female, have to be returned to their origins of life in order to grow up and become conscious of their part in the reproduction of life. Thus reproduction not only belongs to the female sphere of life, which has a significance secondary to the male sphere, but much of public social life is centred on reproduction and is of equal concern to both men and women. Similar conceptualisation to that described here as belonging to the Zaramo is characteristic of other ethnic kin groups in eastern Tanzania with clan descent and inheritance pattern that were originally matrilineal. The women of these societies have had considerable social eminence.

One could advance the tentative hypothesis that the social and physiological concepts of gender and sex in the traditional matrilineal forms of culture have supported the women at a time when a new conceptualisation under more male-oriented social formations has become dominant. The dialectic between the old and the new is a process that still continues today within social and ritual interaction.

Women have a prominent place in rituals related to men and to themselves. First of all they play a part in varying kinship categories as sisters, mothers, mother's and father's sisters and their mothers. They have a variety of specialised tasks as instructors of maturing girls at puberty rituals, as traditional midwives, as healers and diviners, as guardians of famous cult and clan shrines, as specialists in a variety of spirit cults, and as female counterparts to men in communal or family-specific offering rites — which, according to the general pattern of binary symbolism, require in their performance both female and male participation. Even the circumcision of boys could be done by a woman who belonged to the lineage of circumcisors and was initiated to that task. I met two such women, and was myself offered the possibility of being thus initiated for a fee — an offer I declined.

It is not an accident that the guardian of a shrine of historical repute in the eastern Luguru mountains, Kolelo, is a woman. She is of the Mlali clan, and the charge is an inherited one passed on from woman to woman in the family. People from all over the coast, as far as the Mwambao north of Dar es Salaam, speak and sing of Kolelo, and it is one in the continuous pattern of shrines throughout Africa where women are as if the gatekeepers to the sources of continuity in life: they act as a kind of oracle mediating knowledge from past generations through concrete elements of life, water, air and earth. Rain is an outcome, symbolic and concrete of that knowledge.[24] Still in the 1970s, individual petitioners or delegations approached Mlamlali of Kolelo with requests for divining or for esoteric knowledge of healing.[25] The secrets of Kolelo are revealed only to women, whereas men who approach the place with their needs are given answers only through mediating male messengers who serve the distinguished Mlamlali, also referred to as Dibibi. Mlamlali retains the reputation of having to remain unmarried and untouched by men. Men have no hesitation in sending delegations to her when a village is threatened by a common calamity. The causes of delayed rains and other misfortunes are found out at Kolelo and remedies decreed for whole communities; individuals too receive relief from personal distress by finding out the causes of their afflictions. Female adepts also become introduced to some aspects of esoteric knowledge of healing and divining.[26]

I have discussed the visits to Kolelo with villagers in Ukutu, east of the mountains, and with others in Bagamoyo and in Kisarawe Districts. I have also travelled from Bunju, near Dar es Salaam, to Kolelo with one of the leading female diviners and healers, Mwavila binti Shomali, one of the numerous wise counsellors of the coast who was widely known for her extra-sensory capacities of seeing and healing, to ascertain the fame of its influential shrinekeeper. Mwavila also served people even from distant villages who were ill or had misfortune, taking payment which was very small in comparison with the time and energy spent in hours of divining, exorcising, counselling and healing. In her extra hours, she raised crops. After her husband's death, she brought up her two daughters and subsequently kept close contact with them and their children. In her own words, she found no use for another husband, who would only have been a person to be served. She utilised men — characteristically from another ethnic group, the Nyamwezi — for practical chores. Other men acted as assistants in divining sessions, interpreting to the clients the concealed meanings in the songs that expressed social conflicts as the causes of calamity. The male or female assistants also sang the antiphones and amplified the rhythmic shaking of instruments. Such descriptions could be multiplied, since in most of the villages studied there have been leading women practitioners, *waganga*, renowned beyond the borders of one locality.

Skilled diviners such as Mwavila have a keen insight into the social patterns of their society, and bring it to bear in their professional services. They conceive of their task as one given by God, and are aware of their analytical skills. In the case of Mwavila, when the problem at hand transcended her social knowledge, she, like other diviners, did not hesitate to say that she no longer 'saw' the cause. The diviner is the 'sociologist' of a society and her clients recognise her as such.

When Islam, with its centuries-long presence in the coastal villages, began penetrating the interior with the mercantilism of the nineteenth century, it provided an 'alternate' and challenging world view. The coastal social system was not suddenly disrupted, but instead there were gradual transformations from within. The matrilineal clan descent and inheritance became part of a bilineal system. The traditional boys' initiation rites, *ng'hula*, or *vikulege*, became circumcision rites called *jando*. Islamic teachings were woven into traditional mythology; Nyalutanga and Nyapingu were now accompanied by Adam and Hawa (Eve). In the late 1970s both *vikulege* and *jando* were still being performed on boys as separate rituals among the Kucre.[27] With the introduction of Islam, the traditional coastal rituals and practices in which women were prominent were juxtaposed with forms of worship and religious life in which only men had roles. However, both female and male maturity and initiation rituals have retained their symbolic and social significance. *Jando* has been incorporated into the traditional ritual forms, making use of the symbolic themes of older male and female rites. Women are recognised as being significant not only as symbolic figures but as carriers of cultural traditions and agents for the maintenance of historical continuity. They have provided the Zaramo — the original inhabitants of Dar es Salaam — and related coastal people with a sense of historical origin, of security and of identity amidst major social, political and economic changes.

When the people of the coast first met the incoming colonial influences, they resisted being incorporated into the market economy through open rebellions (Bushiri and Maji Maji) and passive unwillingness either to grow cotton for market or to dig gum copal for the ship industry. The Zaramo did not provide the permanent urban labour force as might have been anticipated, especially considering the proportion of their numbers. It appears that the conflict between their own cultural values and those being introduced by colonialists gave the local population a sense of defeat within the new system, to which Zaramo society has given expression by the prevalence of death symbolism in their rituals. Within the coastal societies, presentation culture has become a social force, not only for the preservation of the old, but also for change, even radical change as was the case when Islam was integrated into the traditional cultural system. The change was given expression through the changing emphasis in the symbols inherent in the system.

Throughout the history of the coastal societies, there have been charismatic leaders, many of them women, who have been innovators and creators. Their success has depended on their ability to call on the authority of past generations and on the spirits with whom they were in contact. This is also the context in which the alternate views have been incorporated into new cultural forms and how change has come about. Considering the coastal cultural background, it is not surprising that during the transition to national independence the strongly Islamic society of the Rufiji made room for women in leadership roles in politics. One of them in particular, Bibi Titi, became a well-known politician, and the first President of the women's organisation, UWT. Even within the sphere of religion itself women carved out room for themselves. However, it was uncommon to find women who could recite any parts of the Koran or the *Maulidi* (the story of the birth of the Prophet) even though they had attended Koran schools before reaching puberty. As an exception it was recounted that, particularly in the villages of the Nyagatwa, such as Msindaji in the delta, it was common for women to be able to recite some of the holy books in Arabic. I had a chance to witness this in a funeral ceremony in Ikwiriri, where Binti Ali, wife of a sheikh from Msindaji, conducted a *Maulidi* at a large gathering of women while the men were making the necessary burial arrangements — something which is solely the men's task. Binti Ali was an unassuming woman, with little awareness of her leadership qualities or of her especially high level of learning. She took care of her cooking duties on three stones, just like any other village woman, while at the same time looking after a Koran school with eighteen boys and girls. At the *Maulidi* young women, her earlier students, took part in the reading while others performed the parts in chant as would have been done in any similar celebration conducted by men. A couple of hundred assembled women responded readily. The Koran school under Binti Ali's care was recognised in the name of her husband, whose share was to support his wife in her own learning so that she could manage the demanding task entrusted to her. Not only was she herself unaware of the prestige her performance could have given her, but her neighbours were also unimpressed. When I visited her the first time, the neighbours could not even think whom I might be looking for when I referred to her leadership at the *Maulidi*; only a reference to her husband made the association possible. In this, as in numerous other aspects of women's life, a woman's obvious contribution goes unnoticed or is considered as being in essence that of the man with whom she is associated.

The coastal societies with matrilineal origins have given women an advantage that women in patrilineal societies seldom have, as will be shown later. They never lacked the right to land if land was generally available — a basic fact often ignored when the pros and cons of different lineage systems are discussed in terms of women's rights. Even when land allocations were made by the *kolo*, the leading mother's brother, a woman returning to her lineage area could not be left without a plot to cultivate. More study is needed to clarify to what extent women's ritual significance is associated with their relative material wellbeing. Here I have taken the position that in the changing social situation the coastal people have utilised their *cultural* strength rather than building mainly on material means. However, the right to decide on the use of produce, and the achievement of a degree of surplus are needed before rituals can be perpetuated — which in itself indicates that there is a close connection between the presentational forms of culture and material aspects of life.[29]

At a time when the city of Dar es Salaam has been steadily expanding and usurping traditional land, the cultural means of identity have gained in strength. It is safe to assume that the cultural means whereby change is experienced provide a significant psychological and social force. Through their cultural roles women have retained social eminence, which in many ways is in contrast to the social custom of women's submission generally attributed to Islam. The final authority and power in the society does indeed lie with men, but women have found both authority and power that rest in their culturally acquired qualities. It is not only a few select individuals, but the women of the coast generally who have dressed their problems in a cultural garb, and this has provided an outlet through which they have been able to express their experience of womanhood in relation to the male sex, to the female role in reproduction, to the illnesses with which their lives have been plagued; and to the ever-present threat of death. By being able to give expression to these roles in this way, they have made the life of toil and drudgery bearable. Whenever possible, life has been elevated to a level of celebration, whether savoured in mere porridge of manioc or in pots of beer brewed as a symbolically central ritual element. Maintaining cultural forms of social communication meant sharing considerable portions of food and drink in communal consumption. Women not only worked to produce, they both shaped and enjoyed the social forms of the use of the product. Times of plenty were naturally interspersed with times of severe drought and famine, both past and present, when life became difficult and its excesses were cut down.

After the process of villagisation and the changes in village life it has caused, emphasis has been on production and on construction. This has also tended to impoverish rituals and celebrations. As one *mganga*, a master in therapeutic rituals, put it, 'The spirits will forgive us. They see that we have to build now.' Time will tell what the long term effects will be. In the beginning of the villagisation programme in 1968 severe floods occurred in the Rufiji basin. The people in the valley affected by the waters were moved to the higher ground and settled permanently in new villages. Women describing the events expressed vividly the effects of the calamity on their celebrations (cf. below); they were saying that in that year the Rufiji could no longer sing and dance or celebrate because of their remorse over leaving their homes. The related incident demonstrated the interplay of the material and physical aspects of life with the cultural, presentational forms of tradition.

While social and cultural expressions have been important for women, they also have perpetuated customs detrimental to them. Some of these will be described in the following section, which concentrates on the Rufiji.

Growing up at the River Delta

Until the time of Independence, Rufiji District formed a world of its own. The rising and receding waters of the river had dominated the rhythm of life in the valley for centuries. Disastrous floods were a time-measure by which significant events in people's lives were marked. The story of Binti Mohamedi, the daughter of a prominent Muslim sheikh, *shehe*, in Ikwiriri village, serves here as an illustration of how fully lives were tuned to the rhythm of the river:

I was born at the end of the First World War, when the British and the Germans fought. First was the time of the *konombo* floods, which in Matumbi language means that the waters came to wash away the blood of those who had died in the war. Some people moved up on to higher ground, others climbed up into their stilt-houses.

When the war was over, the waters came again, hot waters, *maji moto*. When they subsided, smallpox came. Two of my brothers died of smallpox. My mother was pregnant with me, and I was born in the valley.

Before I 'matured', there were endless rains, *maji ya lilale*. People only slept, and could not work. I reached womanhood with the Ifakara floods, *maji ya lifakara*. Masses of water rushed down from Ifakara. When the water subsided I was given in marriage.

During the *maji ya yange*, the District Commissioner, John Young, whipped us to make us plant bananas. He took children and looked after them until the famine was over. We didn't like the banana-growing, but the bananas have stayed with us, we don't have famine any more.

Maji ya uhuru were the waters which brought Independence, and then came *maji ya uhamisho*, the floods which moved us to the higher land. That year in our *ngoma* ritual dances our voices dried up in our throats; we only clapped our hands.

I stayed ten years with my first husband, to whom I'd gone after staying secluded for two years.[30] My first pregnancy ended in a miscarriage. The second pregnancy lasted till the seventh month: I didn't cry. The next pregnancy went till the eight month: I cried bitterly. The fourth pregnancy bore a child who cried. He died. I do not have a child. My husband left me. He was no good to me, he cheated me. We had cultivated the land together, but he took what I had worked for.

My second husband came to build a school here. He saw me and married me. We stayed together until he died last year. I haven't married again. I live by myself in my own house, which I built next to the houses of my brother and other relatives.[31]

The story of Binti Mohamedi touches several of the problems women had to face in their lifetime. Among the coastal peasant population in general and particularly in the Rufiji delta, girls were married off somewhere between the ages of twelve and fifteen. The marriage was often arranged much earlier, and the girl could be sent to live in her husband's house even before reaching puberty so that she would get acquainted with the ways of his family and kin. She was then sent back to her father's or mother's house before the ritual celebration of her maturity.[32] This meant that a woman was under her father's protection and care until she was married off, and after the marriage she was looked after and guarded by her husband. In such a position the woman was dependent on the goodwill of the man who was in charge of her, even though some of the life-stories of Rufiji women also tell how they found ways of releasing themselves from such guardianship.

Women may, in their own lives, have rebelled against the relationship of dependence to a man, yet they continued to instruct the *mwali*, young girl, at her puberty rituals, showing no displeasure at the content of the teaching. The girl was told that on going to her husband she must remain quiet and bear her lot; she must not use words or behaviour that would offend him; she must not be stubborn; she must respect her husband's parents as her own; and in all ways conduct herself as an obedient subservient wife. Thus tradition assigned a set of duties which were often in conflict with the new way of life which required women's independent participation in the public life of the villages and towns, in accordance with ujamaa.

Because Islamisation had started earlier and had been more complete in the Rufiji valley than elsewhere in Tanzania, the Koranic schooling had remained the principal educational institution. The few government schools established there in colonial times were promoted with considerable pressure on the parents, at times with vigorous campaigns. The people's resistance towards the Western type of education continued partly because of the fear that with it the people would inadvertently be accepting Christianity also, although the schools were secular government schools. On occasion, under pressure from the authorities, which was particularly felt by those in their service, a lowly government messenger might send his daughter to school, whereas girls of higher social origin were shielded from educational influences. In this way, colonial power played on internal societal contradictions and at times unintentionally benefited the lower-class women as well as men.

The few Rufiji girls who managed to get education beyond a couple of classes in primary school had to be sent out of the area because of the social pressure from their neighbours. In the large village of Ikwiriri only one woman with professional education, the teacher Dawa Salum Mkono, could be located who had originated in the area. A few were known to be working in other parts of the country. Maimuna Saidi's life-story, followed by that of Dawa Salum, will illustrate the seemingly chance factors which affected the lives of the few educated women.

Maimuna Saidi Kihambwe was a nurse employed in a dispensary north of Dar es Salaam where I met her, but she maintained her home in Ikwiriri. The information of her life was given by her son, who was a university student.

Maimuna's father had been a sheikh who saw little benefit in education, least of all for girls. At the age of four, Maimuna was sent to live with her uncle who decided to put her to school. The uncle had been a cook in a European household, had travelled with the family abroad, and had come to appreciate the value of education.

When she was beginning to mature, at the age of twelve, Maimuna was taken out of school and sent back to Rufiji to be secluded. She was then married to a primary school teacher, who helped her to go on informally with education. After a divorce, Maimuna got married to a medical assistant, wo taught her nursing and attending to outpatients. Through a period of service with the Prison Department in a prison dispensary, she was then able to join the service of the Ministry of Health and at the same time provide her own children with education. Both of her two boys were university students.

Life stories of educated men and women from many other parts of the country describe the insistence of mothers on their children's education, often involving great sacrifices on their part. The life of the Rufiji teacher Dawa Salum Mkono is an example of a woman's struggle for a better life for a wider circle of girls than her own children:

Dawa was one of the first girls to go to school in Rufiji. Her father was initially a trader who bought coconuts in Mbwera at the mouth of the river and sold them in Utete, where the Government District Headquarters was. He had gone to school for two years and was later employed by the colonial government as a messenger. In 1947 government employees were urged to send their children to school. Dawa's brother was already too old to go, so it was decided that the girl should be sent to start the first standard. Her father had befriended a European working in Utete, and was thus encouraged to be different from others. However, in 1951 Dawa was the only girl in her class and the pressure on her was too great to continue there. She was sent to Tabora Girls' School to finish her eight-year middle school education, which she ended in 1956. From there she had the chance to continue in a teacher training school, and so she became a teacher. She married and returned to her own home area in Rufiji.[34]

The prevailing opinion still discouraged the girls in many ways from attending school. As one who had gone through the struggle, Dawa Salum fought for those girls who had indicated a desire to continue but were forced by their parents to marry. A case in point was a thirteen-year-old girl in Standard 3. She had stayed away from school for some days, and Dawa heard that she was being married off to an elderly man. Dawa took a policeman with her and went to the place of the celebration. The girl's head had already been shaven, she had been instructed, and she was going to be taken to the husband's house. When asked by the police whether she had willingly agreed to be married, the short answer was 'No'. As a result, the girl was enabled to return to her class and continue school, but she was rejected by her father, who told the teacher: 'Take the child and bring her up.' Dawa managed to find a place for the girl to live and continue her schooling. The teacher commented that in a big village like Ikwiriri it was not so easy to take girls out of school, but in smaller places these things happened more frequently. The parents of another girl prevented her from taking an examination by shutting her in her room when the examination was taking place. In this instance too, the police had to be fetched to force the parents to let the girl go.

In Umwe primary school in Ikwiriri, the numbers of boys and girls starting school were at the time of the study almost equal, 27 and 24. In the third standard the girls were a quarter of the total and in the seventh and last year the girls numbered less than one-sixth. In a sample of nine primary schools in Rufiji in 1973, there were altogether 313 students in the last class, of which 240 were boys and 73 girls. Of the girls at least ten were children or relatives of teachers or other workers from outside the village, which meant that only one-fifth of the pupils in the sampled schools were girls belonging to the village. Until the third year the attendance of both sexes was close to equal, but as girls reached puberty they were marked as having moved away, become pregnant, become ill or as having merely dropped out of school.

Since the implementation of universal primary education in 1978 in Tanzania, it has become harder for parents to take girls out of school and the number of those who continue through the primary school is bound to increase. However, the problem of girls getting pregnant in the upper standards not only interferes with their studies but makes the parents more hesitant to allow the girls to go to school. In other cases, a father may actually encourage a man to make his daughter pregnant in order to get her out of school and in the hope of obtaining some financial advantage. In the year before the interviews with Dawa Salum, three girls in the school where she taught had been dismissed because of pregnancy.[35] Parents could also refuse to buy a uniform for a girl, thereby putting pressure on her and making her school attendance difficult. If there was no precedent in the family for a girl finishing school and going on to further education, the girls themselves had very little incentive to continue their schooling. The only goal that was set for them was marriage.

Women of the River

As the Rufiji woman got older she gained power and authority within the domestic sphere, especially in polygynous households.

She might build up personal wealth and command considerable authority in her own household when the husband divided his attention among several wives. This enabled her to develop her capacity to manage the organisation and even the economy of a household.

At one end of the spectrum in this society there were isolated married élite women, enjoying prestige but condemned to silence in the presence of their male superiors and living a life circumscribed by rules and deprived of personal rights. At the other end were the peasant women. The stricter the adherence to the religious customs of Islam, the more limited was a woman's movement and the more dependent she was on her husband's word, even if such a woman could rise into position within her limited domestic sphere and through it gain social standing.

But whereas wealthier men could afford to place restrictions on their women by sending workers to the fields in their place, ordinary peasants had to leave much of the responsibility of the fieldwork to their wives. This meant hard work for the women, but at the same time it offered them the company of other women and gave them the chance to be away from the village life during the long cultivation season. The season lasted four to five months, during which the women moved to stay in small huts in the fields, particularly when it came to the time to keep the birds and animals away. This pattern became even more pronounced after villagisation.

The freedom the women experienced in their working life, however hard that life might be, found another expression in the rituals through which the women portrayed their joys and sorrows and shared life together. They had institutions in which they had space to move, in which they played significant roles and which they perpetuated with force because the institutions offered them a social field of action. As has already been described, the women played the main roles, in the girls' puberty rites and in therapeutic cults. Otherwise they could participate only selectively in the public life of the village. The possibilities for moving into wider social fields so far belonged to only a few women who had their own sources of income independent from that of their husbands, or who were not tied to a man at all.

Women, as well as men, had access to divorce. A woman who had built up some economic security for herself might simply leave her husband, or make life so miserable for him that he preferred divorce. The woman might be married several times and manage her affairs so that each time she gained some personal benefits, in the form of either money, which she saved, or some other form of material wealth which she could retain at the time of divorce. Whichever method she chose, it is obvious that the Rufiji women had been able to manipulate their situations in such a way that eventually many prefered to stay alone, establishing themselves as independent owners of their own houses and making use of men's services when it was convenient to do so. Thus among the women at the other end of the spectrum there were independent divorced or widowed women, who conducted their economic affairs within the limits that society permitted and who had no intention of giving up the freedom they had achieved, limited as it might be. A growing number of economically independent women came from the peasant class. However, the workload of the poorer peasant woman not only gave her physically demanding tasks to perform, but also responsibility and a sense of skill and knowledge in the realm of production. When in practice a woman carried the responsibility for work, which in public went under her husband's name, she gained the self-confidence to manage the tasks completely alone and for her own benefit. Within the women's community there were several ways in which individual women could manage and share many of their personal difficulties. An example of this was a family in Mohoro made up solely of women in which four generations were living in one housing complex, built by Binti I., who had followed the example of three other women houseowners along the same street. Binti I. had had two husbands but, as she put it: '*Nikachoka, hii bure*, I got tired, this is of no use.' She became weary of them and decided they were of no benefit to her. After leaving them, she could keep the money she made by selling the rice she had cultivated, and paid a man to carry her sacks to the marketplace. The rest of the money was entirely her own. She had a third husband who lived in another village. When the man visited Mohoro, he came and stayed with Binti I., but she felt under no obligation to share any of her money with him. In her own words, she said she was quite independent, taking care of her property and life. Before, life was different: the husband took the money from the rice she cultivated.

Between Binti I. and her mother, the oldest member of the family, there was considerable difference in attitude to life. The mother had been married to a man in the Matumbi hills, and the couple had come down to the Rufiji Valley during the Maji Maji rebellion in 1905. Her husband had been a soldier in the German army and she had travelled all over German East Africa with him; they had lived in Rwanda, Ujiji by Lake Tanganyika and other parts of Tanganyika. It is hard to tell whether the independent attitudes of her grandchildren were a reflection of the wider world outlook she had gained during her travels, since some of her descendants too had settled in different parts of the country. Old as she was, she was still cultivating and her relationship with the younger women was much the same as it must have been with her husband. As she explained: 'They take care of me, they measure the *khanga*, cloth, for me and feed me.'[36] Her grandson and the husband of one of the daughters sold her crop for her and assisted Binti I. in maintaining herself.

But even men turned to the women for assistance. I was present when a man came to Binti I.'s house to ask for her help in a matter which reflected the custom of early marriage. The man had married a young girl before she had reached maturity whom he already called his wife. When she began menstruating she had been secluded as custom demanded, and it was the duty of the husband to find the means to pay the required bridewealth. This man had already paid a part of it at the time he made the agreement with her parents, and later added more. Altogether he had paid 250 Tanzanian shillings, and now he wanted the remaining 120 shillings to get the girl out of seclusion and asked Binti I. to lend him 30 or 40 shillings. He remarked to me, 'These are people whom I depend on.' When I asked him why he did not have money himself to pay for his wife, he said that he had no work. When questioned why he did not cultivate rice to get money, his reply was 'Rice is women's work.' Because women were accustomed to working, they could become known as people with means when they lived independently. For men living without the support of women's labour this was much harder.

It is significant that most of the women in leadership positions, especially in the Coast Region, were independent from men. In all cases they had at some stage been married, since in the Tanzanian context the word 'woman' in itself signified a married woman in the traditional sense. The chairwoman of the local Women's Union of Tanzania (UWT) in Mbwera, Binti A., was an example of such a woman. She belonged to the older families of Mbwera; her grandfather had built the mosque there and had planted coconut trees around the village. She herself built a house in Dar es Salaam after her husband left her and she owned another house in Mbwera, where she was now living. She had one son living with her and was continuing to cultivate. She was not wealthy, but seemed to get along quite well.

Women had often gained their independence after a personal struggle which had left them initially at a disadvantage. They had gradually become aware of the injustices they faced and of their deprived position in life. Binti K.'s case, also in Mbwera, was a good example of this. In her own words:

Your husband sends you off to work in the fields. You work on your own fields and those of your husband. While you are there he takes your stored crops, goes and sells them and buys coconuts which are his. You are on the fields for months, and when you come home you find that he has taken another woman with the money you have provided for him. The one who worked does not eat the benefits of her work; another person eats it.

There are those women who want to have control over their own share. One who agrees to have her share taken does not get anything. It does not pay to bring your problems to the elders, who are men. Women never get anything from them. The argument goes, 'You have worked together, so you share the benefits, and the husband looks after your wealth. So it is his right to do what he sees fit.'

This is the way it is in the villages — husbands are not at all fair. Some men take your rice and rent coconut trees with the money and then sell the coconuts. In some cases, the husband may even sell the things that you have in your house, and you don't get any other food to eat but that which you produce from your own fields.

Binti K. was the representative of Mbwera women in the Regional and District Party conferences. She had nine adult children. She and her husband had cultivated sugarcane, bananas and oranges and had kept goats in Mohoro. This was the basis of the wealth on which she later built her own house, despite her complaint that her husband had made use of most of what they had accumulated. She now managed her own affairs, running a teahouse where her customers were men, since only men could walk around the village at leisure. Yet Binti K. made the point that she, like women in general, had to send their 'children' to sell their crops, since they themselves were not supposed to appear in public places.

The rules of conduct relating to women were in practice full of contradictions. Changes in society created a new situation in which the old rules no longer applied. Thus one of the shopkeepers in Mbwera was a married woman, but she had no complaints against her husband; he let her manage her business without interference. She had gained her investments through her own hard work after having been married earlier and later divorced. She had started a shop and was doing well when a Primary Court magistrate moved into the village and married her. The wife did not support her husband, who managed with his own salary. This was an example of a case where an arrangement had been achieved which satisfied both parties and which gave the woman an opportunity to be both a wife and an income-earner with her own independent sphere of activity.

It is significant that all the women whose situation has been described as giving them personal satisfaction had reached such a state only after gaining income apart from their husbands, for activities in which they could use their own abilities. If the women who had thus gained a degree of independence became conscious of the power they exercised, they could influence matters so that they would not be treated as inferiors in public affairs, since men's *de facto* dependence on them was manifested in many different ways. Obviously women needed an increased awareness of the potential they had possessed to make use of the means at their disposal.

In the traditional villages a very general concensus of opinion was expressed, among both men and women, that 'Women do not participate in communal efforts related to nation-building or politics.' Opinions differed as to why this was so. In the local party committees, at least one member had to be a woman, and there had to be one woman among the village representatives to District and Regional party meetings. When asked why representation was allotted to one woman only, a Party Divisional Secretary replied: 'We are giving them a lot of thought, but the circumstances are not easy. They have not yet had political awakening.' Divisional political and administrative leaders seemed to think that the women did not take part in politics because of their lack of understanding and interest. One village chairman referred to women villagers as *wanaomilikiwa*, the dominated ones, when explaining why they had no direct village membership. Women were dominated by their husbands. They had to obtain permission from their husbands in order to take part in common activities, and were often prevented by them from doing so. However, there were more women attending the literacy classes, because learning to read was more or less obligatory. Some men claimed that public activity by women would lead to unfaithfulness to their husbands, and the women themselves maintained that the main reason why women did not attend public meetings was the men's fear of their wives' possible unfaithfulness.

Observation confirmed that the women's lives were filled by work, and by preparation for common social events that could not be neglected. The men, on the other hand, could come and go as they pleased; they lived in the village itself, not in the fields. Many went to the mosque twice a day or more, and passed their time in conversation or in organised business transactions. Some men were labourers engaged in the felling or shelling of coconuts and the making of copra, while others were involved in fishing. But men mostly had more time and fewer obligations than the women and could therefore attend the political meetings.

In a village discussion, a woman vividly illustrated the women's problematic position, which she claimed had its origins in the 'Arab colonialism' of the coastal peoples. The women, she said, had tried lifting the 'colonialism' that continued to oppress them, but their timidity could be compared with that of the turtle, an animal which puts out its head from under its protective shell but pulls it in again quickly for fear that its head will get cut off! At times women were also suspicious of one another, and such mutual discord was cited as a cause for women's inability to organise themselves. When money collections were made and the person holding the purse was suddenly seen wearing a new *khanga*, suspicions were immediately aroused as to the source of the money. Such matters caused back-biting, and meetings arranged by such women ceased to be attended; the women leaders in question defended themselves, became embittered and gave up their leadership, especially when they knew that they had not misused the funds in their charge.

When women were encouraged to participate in meetings, it was because high-level visitors from outside, such as District and Regional Party Secretaries, were visiting. On such rare occasions, women were asked, among other things, to provide the cheering crowd that was needed to make a good impression. Again the women were needed for celebration.

The Rufiji women's participation in politics under the leadership of Bibi Titi during the struggle for independence had not left any obvious or visible traces at the local level, other than perhaps the prescribed women's presence at Party committees. But another way in which women had begun to play a public role was with the establishment of the local branches of the women's organisation, UWT. However, organising women in the context of prevailing contradictions had not been without difficulties, and an example of this is provided by the setting up of the UWT in Mbwera under Binti A.'s leadership. Since Mbwera was unreachable by road, and a boat trip from the District Headquarters in Utete took a day and a night because of the changing tides, it was very seldom visited by any officers from Headquarters; hence the UWT had been operating on its own. After it had been organised, the members had grown a vegetable garden and given the money from its produce to the local clinic to build a house for the Rural Medical Aid. Later, inertia set in; no activity followed the initial efforts, and the UWT was no longer even holding meetings. This the women attributed partly to members having fallen ill or died, and partly to their heavy work-load in cultivation: staying in the fields far from the village during the cultivation season prevented the kind of cooperative activities that called for constant working together in the village. The village had had plans for starting up a cooperative shop, and for sheep herding and cattle keeping. Meetings had taken place, but the plans had not got under way. Binti A. emphasised several times that many cases of illness and many deaths in the village had given the women a lot of extra work in food preparation and ritual activity, apart from their regular chores, so that they could not extend their efforts to any other cooperatives ventures, in the context of either the UWT or the village.[37]

Several attempts had been made in other villages of Rufiji District to get UWT and other cooperative activities under way. In Ikwiriri the UWT handled the catering for a large government seminar, and the money earned from this helped the women to open a teahouse. The women volunteered to cook food in the '*hoteli*' for a small sum of pocket money; however, this soon became a burden because cultivation took up so much of the women's time. Only a few women continued, and did so more or less for their own private gain. Apart from the long time spent in the fields, additional time was taken up by various initiation rituals, *ngoma*, which started right after the harvest and lasted for weeks in August and September. And in Muslim communities Ramadhan, the month of fasting, was a time when women could not participate in public affairs; their major work during Ramadhan was to prepare the evening and night feasts (meals eaten after fasting the whole day). Very little time or strength was left over for cooperative activities.

Externally promoted income-producing activities for women were equally unsatisfactory. Poultry projects had operated for a period, but then either chicken feed could no longer be obtained, or chickens died off from disease. When the women had been assisted to grow vegetables as cash crops, the necessary seeds were soon not available through the agricultural officers, whose duty it was to provide them. Most of the vegetables that the women did manage to grow alongside the school garden were eaten by the school's herd of goats and cows due to the negligence of a pupil on duty. The young women were also disappointed when the sewing machines, which had been promised for school leavers by a women's organisation, failed to turn up. The only thing left for women to do was to keep on growing rice on individual plots as they had always done. But in many of the villages even that became harder when the distance from the new villages to the river plains became too long for the care of the paddy fields to be maintained. According to a BRALUP study made in 1974, the estimated income of Ngorongo villagers decreased by half because of the change in cultivated crops in the new location.[38]

The changes in society brought very few visible benefits for women in Rufiji District, and the result was that the younger women in particular tended to migrate to town. The demands to which women were subjected grew excessively. The development planning which was executed was not realistic; it was not based on knowledge of the women's actual situation, nor did it build on their potential strength. It was partly the attitudes of the male population and partly the failure of the administration to recognise how over-burdened the women were with productive and cultural duties which hampered both the full contribution that women could make in political and developmental activities and their full potential impact in production.

Women and witches

The contradictory forces historically operating in Rufiji were in one way or another reflected in the practice of witchcraft, which was commonly believed to be rampant in the area and at the same time is an aspect of life there which is relatively unexplored, since it is concealed in a garb of traditional beliefs. It touches the lives of women in a tragic way. At least twice in the 1960s the High Court of Tanzania handled witchcraft cases from Rufiji which ended in the execution of several women, while on each occasion there was a man connected also with the case who went free for lack of evidence.

The alleged witchcraft practices of Rufiji have given it a bad name. Fear of such practices has caused university students to shun work in the area, and even those living there spoke about it with great apprehension. The information from the cases tried in the High Court showed that there were groups of women organised in covens of some kind, operating under an obligation that each member in turn would provide a member of their kin as a victim for the purposes of the cult group. Little is known of the practice, but from knowledge of comparable practices among the Wanji along the upper reaches of the same river far inland, which are part of a fertility cult, I surmise that in Rufiji too the women's activities are connected with fertility and go far back into the past.

The pattern in such cults is similar: a group of closely-knit people are bound by oath to an inherited obligation to continue to provide the needed ingredients for the preparation of fertility medicine. Failure to conform brings death. Hypnosis often plays a part, with the victim going under its influence to a place where he or she is mutilated, losing certain parts of the body. Such a deed, if it results in the victim's death, is punishable by death according to the witchcraft ordinance in Tanzanian law. To my knowledge, very little has been done to research the plight of women who have fallen victim to this macabre practice. However, with knowledge of the social organisation and with evidence that a man has been involved in each case, it is reasonable to assume that through fear of the consequences a break from tradition might have for them, the women have been subjected to the practice under the control of male leaders. In such a case, the utilisation of the medicine prepared from the victims' bodily extremities would be in the hands of male cult leaders and the practice would be limited to certain clans. During this study certain fertility rituals were still being performed by members of a specific clan in the area of Mpima village at the start of the cultivation season, and again at harvest time. It could not be ascertained whether it had any connection with the practice of witchcraft.[38]

My hypothesis, for which the evidence is insufficient at this point, is that this kind of witchcraft is practised in order to prepare medicine for agricultural use and possibly for use in puberty rituals for fertility. It may well have developed as an expression of power and necessary control over unpredictable natural forces, and it may also have provided a force to counteract the foreign *elimu ya dunia* (secular Islamic learning) of the local aristocracy, and thus of course their social and economic dominance. Women's peripheral role in controlling the economy has made them victims in the witchcraft practice itself and in the prosecution of specific cases of witchcraft. Because of an unanalysed tradition which is too sensitive an issue to be approached, women have been suspected of being witches within the Rufiji societies and have been publicly convicted in the absence of adequate understanding of how such a cult works. Witchcraft beliefs are among the clearest examples of traditional beliefs being used to perpetuate specific, carefully chosen elements of tradition in the present-day strife between competing forces. That women become the central figures in this strife is evidence that their traditional roles still have a central bearing.

Summing up

The strength of the coastal women is in their contribution to production for the subsistence of their families and for sale. However, their share in productive work has become excessive. Since colonial times it has been utilised within the wider society to support the official employment structure with unremunerated female labour. Men control this labour, but because of men's prolonged absences women have found ways of gaining relative independence for themselves and using that position for leadership.

Women are also carriers of a rich cultural heritage which they express in many ritual celebrations for the socialisation of the young and for the healing of disease within the traditional symbolic system. The symbols can become expressions of built-in conflicts, working themselves into an Islamic form of 'secular learning' and being utilised as a vehicle of sorcery in changing situations in which social relations are undefined. Thus strength, whether related to productive or to symbolic forces, can be turned to strain. The aim of this chapter has been to demonstrate that it is possible for women to become aware of their own resources and to make increasing use of them, and not just to be pushed aside or crushed under the pressure to which they are subjected. Change may cause disruption in established social systems and break established relationships. Woman's independence, her control over her own life, has been emphasised. It has been shown that within the society there are historical roots which have continued to support women in their struggle, but that the cultural resources from which they can gain support, also have an effect at times which is detrimental to their lives.

NOTES

1. Wright, 1975, 800–19.
2. Church Missionary Intelligence, 1882/8, 478.
3. Information to author, 1965, from Salum Mhunzi, whose son-in-law was a bar-owner at Kwa Binti Madenge, Buguruni, Dar es Salaam, and who lived in Bunju, on the way to Bagamoyo from Dar es Salaam.
4. Weule, 1909, 186, 282.
5. Bachhofen, 1926; Engels, 1976, 36; e.g. Evelyn Reed.
6. R. Young and H. Fosbrooke, 1960, 43–51.
7. Katoke, 1970; Bryceson and Mbilinyi, 1978.
8. Beidelman, 1962, 18.
9. Kjekshus, 1977, 58–9; Iliffe, 1979; *Bulletin Général*, 1877, 80.
10. Meinhof, 1914, 131–3.
11. Beidelman, 1962, does not mention the Kwere among the raiders. Information to author from Kwere elders in Chalinze, 1966. UTAF 1977/12. Also in Utafiti wa Maofisa Utamaduni, Miono 1977, 115. Information from Mboga.
12. Swantz interview 1966, UTAF 1977/12, Utafiti wa Maofisa 1977, 115, Beidelman, ibid.
13. Baur, 1882, 14.
14. Swantz, 1973, 6.
15. Sitari, 1979.
16. Iliffe, 1979, 120.
17. By ritual is meant a series of rites through which a group of people express their basic conseptualisation of life in a symbolic way within a social context. Swantz, 1970, 44.
18. Swantz, 1972, 96–117. Myth as a concept belongs to Western thought patterns. Myths of origin within the coastal cultures are used to relate a symbolic, ritual act to the natural or historical origins of the people who perform it. For the fuller treatment of concepts of symbol and ritual, cf. Swantz, 1970, 44–57.
19. Ibid., 109.
20. Ibid., 112–14.
21. E.g. the Kwere, information from Roweza, Lugoba, and Timotheo Joseph, Mandera; UTAF; the Zaramo *et al.* traditions about the

skirmishes with the Kamba (e.g. L. Swantz, 1965; Feiermann, mimeo).

22. Swantz, 1976, 144.
23. For full description see Swantz, 1970.
24. Birgit Åkesson, with whom I did fieldwork at times, has given this process an artist's interpretation in her book, 1983, 222–3.
25. Iliffe, 1979; L. Swantz 1965 and 1977; M.-L. Swantz, 1970; inf. from Ukutu, MLS 1966; Bunju 1965–75; Kolelo, 1968, MLS, and Dar es Salaam 1969, LS. Mlamlali means 'daughter of one whose clan is Mlali'.
26. Mwavila binti Shomali, 1968 and 1975, MLS. Mwavila died in 1983.
27. M.-L. Swantz, 'Zaramo Jando Rites in the Mwambao Area', Research Reports, Institute of Sociology. University of Helsinki, no. 190, 1973. Also Swantz, 1972, 111.
28. Swantz, 1970.
29. It is shown later that a single or divorced woman has more independence and control over her produce than a married woman. A ritual context also gives the married woman an opportunity to use both cash and produce according to ritual requirements. This is not always noticed when women's rights are analysed.
30. The seclusion of a young girl at the time of physical maturation is customary in the coastal cultures of Tanzania. It could formerly last some months or even years, but nowadays is shortened to one week or a few weeks.
31. Told to the author in Ikwiriri, 14.4.1973.
32. The legal minimum age of marriage is now 15 years for a woman and 18 for a man.
33. Information from Maimuna Saidi's son, 1975.
34. Information from Dawa Salum, June 1974.
35. In Lugoba ward in Bagamoyo District, during the period of Jipemoyo research, 120 cases of schoolgirl preganancies were handled at the Primary Court, an average of 30 per year (1975–9). Information by Jonas Wanga.
36. *Khanga* is the Swahili word for a pair of colourful cloths that women wrap around themselves and use as their everyday apparel. It was the husband's duty to provide his wife with *khangas*.
37. Therapeutic events as well as funerals require extensive rituals, as I have had the opportunity to witness. In addition, the preparation of food for the assembled people is done by women, apart from some Islamic ritual food.
38. Report of a university student, C. Bangaki, from Mpima, 1973.

2

WOMAN AS THE PRODUCER AND PROVIDER IN BUKOBA DISTRICT

Focus on the Haya

Historical Perspective

Bukoba District contains some of the most densely populated areas of Tanzania. The population, mainly of ethnic groups of Haya identity, is clustered, centring in the most fertile areas along the hills west of Lake Victoria-Nyanza and west and southwest of Bukoba town, where small pockets have a density of up to almost 1,500 people per square kilometre (Rudengren, 1974, 4). Westwards, the density decreases and parts of the country have been almost totally uninhabited. The clustering of the population has created an acute land shortage in the District.

The land shortage became acute through a landowner-tenant system called *nyarubanja*, rooted in historical differences between ruling immigrant clans which lived from pastoralism, and others who were cultivators. With the authority of cattle ownership and superior mystic powers, the immigrant clans made the cultivators dependent on them through a system of exchange of produce and services. Some clans usurped power over others, developing eventually into small kingdoms, in which ultimate claim over all the land was in the hands of kings who could redistribute it as favours to distinguished clan leaders. Towards the end of the nineteenth century a disastrous cattle disease finally forced the cattle owners to become dependent on land. Former cultivators were made tenants on their own soil. Portions of land were occupied under a feudalistic system whereby the tenants were expected to pay tribute to their landlords, and had no permanent rights to the ground they cultivated. The tenants' access to land was entirely dependent on the goodwill of the landlords (Egero, 1974, 21; Hyden, 1968, 78).

Systematic taxation was introduced by the Germans in 1904. One-third of the taxes had to go to the chiefs. The *nyarubanja* tenants found the payment of taxes difficult, since these were in addition to the tribute they were already paying to the landlords. This turned their position into plain serfdom. In 1936 there was an official abrogation of the power to create new *nyarubanja* holdings, but the old obligations were maintained until the official abolition of the system in 1967 (Hyden, 1968, 98).

Those who were pushed off the land formed the basis for extensive labour migration to Uganda and elsewhere. In 1969 there were 54,000 Tanzanian-born migrants in Uganda, among whom the Haya were well represented. Two-thirds of those Tanzanian immigrants were men and one-third were women (Egero, 1974, 10). The contact of the Haya with Uganda had old roots through common origins and clan relationships. Numbers of Ganda had migrated to Bukoba District in the nineteenth century during the Ugandan civil wars (Hyden, 1968, 97). Before the turn of the century, men and even women were already going to Uganda in search of work and new opportunities. On their return they brought back new religious influences in the form of Christianity and Islam (Sundkler, 1974). The opening of the railway in 1902 from the coast to Port Florence, now Kisumu (Johnston, 1902, 267), increased trade between the trading posts around Lake Victoria, and the coming of the steamer in 1904, navigating between the major ports, made possible movement of people on a new scale.

The improved trade links accelerated the growing of cash crops, and this development was encouraged by the German rulers. Emin Pasha, the resident representative of the German colonial authorities in Bukoba, established a large coffee nursery there with the intention of distributing young plants to local cultivators, so breaking down the chief's monopoly on coffee-growing (Moffett, 1958, 193; *A Handbook of German East Africa*, 1916, 282). However, as the land was in the hands of the ruling clans, commercial coffee-growing accelerated the inequality between the various classes. Male dominance over the female was also strengthened. Even a tenant paying tribute to the landowner had his own underling in his wife. After coffee became every man's crop, the man was taught how to care for it; consequently he also kept the income from it, while the wife grew the food crops. In the tenant families the woman's strength was heavily taxed to provide the household necessities as well as the share for tribute. In some tenant households women took over men's work while the men fulfilled their duties towards the landlord or chief, or went into other employment to earn the tax money.

The power invested in chiefs and extended by them to the upper-class landholders affected the women's position in Haya society. Not only did it create an impoverished class of tenant women with double labour demands, but it also contributed to the formation of the concept that a woman can be used as an economic or social commodity for exchange.

The customs of the kings and ruling classes of the neighbouring Nyambo in Karagwe closely resemble those which Cory, a government sociologist, attributed to the Haya. Israel Katoke remarks that daughters were an asset to a family, making a man with many daughters rich (Katoke, 1975, 75-6; Cory and Hartnoll, 1945). A chief could oblige his subjects to give him their daughters as slave girls for specific reasons. Katoke gives these and three additional ways in which slaves, mostly girls, were detained in private homes or at the king's palace in Karagwe:

1. Captors were allowed by the king (*Mukame*) or generals to keep some war captives. Some were taken by the king and the generals themselves, some by other superior officers of the army;
2. Wealthy people could buy slaves from slave owners;
3. If heavily fined, a man could retain his civil liberty by sending his daughters to the court;
4. When a subject was allotted land by a king the man sent one of his daughters to the king as a slave girl, as a sign of his gratitude;
5. When a man died childless, his sister sent her daughter to the king;
6. A special fee was paid, usually in the form of a girl, for permission to bury a man executed by the king;
7. Wealthy persons and kings sent slaves to friends, relatives and fellow kings as gifts, to become wives or servants;
8. Parents offered their children, particularly daughters, in exchange for food in times of famine;
9. Slaves were also acquired through inheritance (Katoke, *ibid.*).

The Haya chiefs had full rights over the girls and could dispose of them in any way they wanted. A slave girl given to a friend as a present or for service could rise to the status of a wife or remain as a slave or concubine. Even when taken as a wife she could still be treated like any commercial product, at the sole will of the owner. Such girls were then used to cultivate the chief's land in various villages. The daughters of such a woman remained in the same position as their mother, but the daughters of sons of such women did not retain slave status.

Apart from the tribute system of slave girls, girls could also be pledged by the father for a loan of 20-60 shillings, whereby the girl went to live in the creditor's house. If the creditor had sexual intercourse with the girl, the bridewealth that he then paid for her cancelled out the father's debt, or the debt was deducted from the bridewealth. If the girl ran away, or if she died, the loan repayment became due (Cory and Hartnoll, 1945, 228).

It seems obvious that there were inbuilt ways in the system whereby the young girls were treated as commodities for exchange. Marcia Wright has shown in her studies of women in East-Central Africa that 'in times of extreme crisis men raised capital by disposing of low-status women' (Wright, 1974, 20). In the feudal

Haya society this kind of disposal of women developed almost into an institution and continued over a long period of time. In the similar cases which Marcia Wright describes from southern Tanzania, the women in question had to seek male protectors in order to survive within the social realities of the rural society of their time. Haya women were also taken to bustling trading centres on the Lake, or accompanied their temporary male protectors to the Coast. The urban societies in which they established themselves did not operate within the status system of a rural society, and could accommodate women who offered their sexual services to men from varying racial and ethnic backgrounds.

When the chiefs established trade links with traders outside Haya country, it can be assumed that, given the prevailing system, the use of low-status women was one of the main ways of showing favours to outsiders. Although it has been said that Haya have never been sold as slaves, the contacts of their chiefs with Nyamwezi, Swahili and Arab traders in the early nineteenth century included the exchange of domestic slaves, and the practice of slavery was certainly known in the area. The Germans intercepted a number of slave traders crossing the country with Ganda women and children, who were then put into the care of the White Fathers, the main Roman Catholic order working in the area (Moffett, 1958, 68). In the neighbouring Kagera the explorers Speke and Grant were in 1862 offered some slaves of King Rumanyika (Katoke, *ibid.*).

The German officers and their African troops who were stationed in Bukoba were among the foreigners whose presence from 1890 onwards may have encouraged gift exchanges including the services of Haya women, whose grace and beauty were praised by the Germans (Stuhlmann, 1894, 716). An old Haya man is quoted by Southall as having witnessed how Haya women were in demand by the Germans posted in Bukoba[1] (Southall-Gutkind, 1957, 82). Johnston describes the population which followed the railway to Port Florence as being a mixture of nationalities and races. The opening of the railway facilitated the flight of the Haya women from their home areas, making Mombasa one of the main centres of their migration.

The old people in Bukoba, however, maintained that in older times there were no prostitutes (Gustafsson, 1972, 47), and Rehse mentions in his book that in this time (1910, 96) there were no Haya prostitutes but that there were Ganda who came to Haya country and practised prostitution. It is likely that Haya prostitution started in such covert ways as through a system of exchange, so that the exact time of its beginnings cannot be determined. It accelerated after the First World War when European men came in greater numbers to East Africa (Gustafsson, 1972, 48). From Haya country there was easy access to Uganda and Kenya, as well as to other parts of Tanganyika, through the steamer and rail services, more so than from any other part of Tanganyika. The same chiefs who had practised exchanging women as favours witnessed commercialisation of their women's services.

Concern over prostitution arose from the complaint that men found their wives leaving for the towns, and there were no legal powers to prevent this (Hyden, 1969, 109–10). The first indigenous political organisation, the African Association, felt that prostitution could be brought to an end by making prostitutes pay taxes on their earnings. This problem led the same Association to write a letter to the Council of Chiefs in 1933, urging the equal rights of inheritance for women (Hyden, *ibid*.).

In the current position of women in Haya society, therefore, several strands can be traced historically. The social demarcations resulting in distinct social classes were so extreme that members of certain families from different social levels would not even eat together. A man could take a woman from a lower clan as a wife, as a tribute payment, or as a pawn in a loan transaction. In such a case her status was an individual one — the man's family was not connected to her family, and thus there did not need to be any reciprocal obligations between the families. So the woman was unsupported. The arbitrary powers of the chiefs, the development of serfdom, land shortage and labour migrations, the use of women as a means of exchange, and the invariable control of cash crops by men — all these are vital contributory factors in the development of the women's situation.

Women as producers

The woman's basic role in the Haya, as in many other Tanzanian societies, has been to produce and to reproduce, providing family subsistence and continuity of the husband's clan. If the woman successfully performs these roles, the chances are that she can stay throughout her lifetime in the husband's homestead, even if she eventually becomes one of several wives, or is widowed. Divorce, however, has been a common occurrence, as will be seen later.

The woman's role as producer is here discussed on the basis of data from Kangabusharo, Lugaze and two Bugabo villages, and comparisons with other previous studies. Additional descriptive material is taken from Kilimelile, established as a new ujamaa village at the beginning of the 1970s.

Sample from Kangabusharo and Lugaze. From two villages about 16–20 km. away from Bukoba town, a sample of 30 women and their families was selected for closer observation, representing different age, marital and economic groups. Ten were from the traditional Lugaze and twenty from the neighbouring Kangabusharo villages. At the time of the study the sample represented 9% of the Lugaze and 30% of the Kangabusharo women. All were Haya by ethnic background. Kangabusharo was partly an ujamaa village, and 12 women in the sample were ujamaa members, representing 44% of all the women who had joined the ujamaa village. The 30 women are here treated as one sample except for a few factors in which comparison between the traditional village and ujamaa village is significant.[2]

With regard to education, 17 of the sample had none, 13 had lower primary and 4 had upper primary school education. One had had four years in a secondary school.

Twenty out of the 30 in the sample were married, 5 were widows and 5 were divorced. Of the husbands 6 were fulltime farmers. Other husbands' occupations included teaching, office work, driving and shopkeeping. Of the present husbands 6 were working in town. Thus the families of the interviewed married women were not solely dependent on farm income. Other occupations in which husbands were engaged temporarily or permanently also reduced men's participation in farming activities, leaving more and more of the work for the women.

The average number of children born to these women was 3.8. All divorced women who had borne children had some children living with them. This may indicate a change in men's attitudes towards the custom which dictates that men keep the children after divorce. Three women had no children: one of them was divorced, and one had married three times and was living as the fifth consecutive wife of her present husband. One was the wife of a church worker. Five women had their husband's children from previous marriages living with them.

The 20 married women were living in their husband's houses. Half of them were living with their in-laws in neighbouring houses and an additional three with other clan members. Three widows had grandchildren with them and one continued to live in her in-laws' homestead. Three of the 5 divorced women were living in their father's house (2 of the fathers were divorced from the informants' mothers). In two of these fathers' homes there were hired servants in the household. Two of the 3 divorced women had children there with them; 4 widows and two of the divorcees lived in their own houses, one of the latter next to her brothers.

One widow continued to occupy her former husband's house but cultivated her own field. Six other divorcees and widows had their own fields and two divorcees cultivated on their father's fields. Other women cultivated land which belonged to their husbands (on two, no information). The average size of the cultivated area for those for whom information was available was given as 1.7 acres. (On nine, no information; three described as small only. In Lugaze the average size was 2.2 acres, in Kangabusharo 1.4 acres, for the non-ujamaa 2.2 acres.) According to Priscilla Reining, a minimum viable unit for successful cropping in the 1950s was one acre. Today one acre can hardly support a family without other income. This must be one important reason why more women engage in *misiri* cultivation than before.[3]

All 28 women of whom information about crops grown was given grew bananas, and all but one also grew coffee. Other crops grown were tea, beans, potatoes, groundnuts, cassava and a few other odd crops such as pineapple. Four were reported as growing no food crops besides bananas. Two of them were too old and two were wives of a teacher and of an office worker in town. It was said that the reason why so few had grown groundnuts was that the local chief had forbidden it that year. There were men and women who still offered free labour once a month on the chief's farm, since they believed that the prosperity of their crops depended on the goodwill of the chief.

The Bugabo villages

A Bugabo village was studied in detail and additional interviews were conducted in its neighbouring village. These villages will not be referred to by name because of the personal nature of the information.

Four separate surveys were made, involving
1. 30 households covering the total area of one part of the village;
2. 15 women who had returned from prostitution and settled in the village;
3. 13 women living in or next to their brothers' households; and
4. 14 divorcees and widows.

The information from Bugabo concentrated on questions related to women's personal history and thus does not contain detailed agricultural data, only the general agricultural pattern.

Village R. consists of about 100 households with an average of $1\frac{1}{2}$ acres of land. One-third of the houses kept cattle, an average of 4 cows, some having up to 9 and others only 1 or 2. Cattle-keeping had been encouraged, and the veterinary services had been improved.

There was a cattle dip a mile away. The village cattle were taken out to graze as one herd by members of households or by hired labourers of the cattle-keepers in turns, and were returned to the homestead for the night. Men were responsible for the livestock in general. It was their task to take the cattle out, to bring grass, to milk and to milkfeed the calves. Women cleaned the shed, spread the manure and looked after the calves.

The farms with cattle had better flourishing plantain (cooking banana) and coffee plantations than the farms without the steady supply of manure. Plantains and bananas were grown in the area next to the house, leaving a wide entrance opening free from any cultivation. This was used for drying coffee, thrashing beans and for any other work or celebration requiring space. Plantains were inter-cropped with beans once a year, this also increasing the fertility of the field. Coffee was grown in a separate area in the outer circle around the house. Some coffee and plantain intercropping could also be seen. Some farmers had taken tea as a new cash crop, but households already using their maximum land and labour capacity had not found it possible to take up tea-growing. An important crop grown in the village area and outside it on the *misiri* land was sweet potato, but hardnuts and groundnuts were the most common crops of the *misiri* cultivation, as well as yams. Cassava had also become more and more common, especially since the government had encouraged the growing of it as a drought crop.

Women had started selling some of their *misiri* crops when they had had a good harvest. A woman in R. said that she had got 400 shillings this way. It was difficult to get accurate figures, partly because the women did the selling little by little and did not add up their earnings, and partly because they were unwilling to reveal the amounts. They used the money for buying clothes and other necessities. The woman referred to above could spend more time on her cultivation because she was not living with her husband. She had no children herself and had been taking care of her brother's chil-dren. Thus the money was needed for the daily expenditure at home, as well as for clothing. Marketing of the *misiri* crops had not been organised, and women could sell only when there was a ready market for their produce. The women lack practice in marketing, and it takes a long time for their trade to get established. As things stand, transportation is in the hands of men, and the men are only interested in organising transport when it is profitable for them-selves. Unless systematic attention is given to women's marketing activities, the benefits of larger-scale trading will go into the pockets of the transporters, with women reaping a bare minimum.

The diet consisted of *ebitoke*, banana cooked with either meat or beans. Fish was also eaten, and some of the men in the village were part-time or full-time fishermen. No detailed study was made to find out how this general description of diet corresponded to the diet of the poorer households. Presumably the division between cattle-owners and those without cattle resulted also in diet differences.

The division of work within the household followed the general pattern in the district. Men took care of the coffee and banana/plaintain fields, but in many households women frequently did men's work. Men brewed the beer, but even then the women did all the preparatory work: collecting the bananas; digging the hole in the ground where the ripe bananas are left to ferment; carrying the necessary water, grass and banana leaves; and preparing the calabashes. Only the actual pressing of the bananas, which is done with the feet, was left to the men.

The social stratification in the village followed the size and number of the fields, the number of coffee trees, the number of cattle, and the occupations managed apart from cultivation and animal husbandry. In some cases contributions were made by relatives working outside the village. In the villages studied, there were only a few signs of outside investment in the better-standard buildings and extended cultivation which could be seen in many other parts. The standard of housing revealed rather well the economic levels of the villagers, a good proportion of whom lived in traditional grass-covered or round mud-and-stick houses. Much more investigation is needed to analyse the differences in the lives of women from these different strata.

The pattern of women's activities

Priscilla Reining's study of the Haya in the 1950s claimed that men and women are equally engaged in cultivation, men taking care of the banana and coffee plantations and women the food crops, with both using only a few hours of the morning for this (Reining, 1952, 47–51). The Kangabusharo-Lugaze pattern of work did not confirm this claim, and neither did observation of life in the Bugabo area. It was very general that women worked longer hours and were engaged in work in the fields for much longer periods than men. The food crops grown outside the actual village area on *misiri* land often require a long walk to and from the fields, and the work can be strenuous. Only occasionally were men seen working in these fields, mainly clearing the land in preparation for the women's daily toil. Studies made by Jorgen and Karen Rald show in detail the division of labour between men and women. In the majority of households, women's agricultural work considerably exceeds that of men (Rald,

1975, 78). Men often have some form of employment or self-employment outside the farm. Observations about the men's work-load have concerned those engaged supposedly in full-time farming. Outside employment may not be full-time, but can be sufficient to excuse a man from farm work. Such half-time jobs were for example that of the chairman of the village, the clerk of the Cooperative, the dispensary assistant, a driver and a casual labourer.

According to Reining, one expression of the complexity of Haya society and its peasant nature, as compared with other rural or 'tribal' societies with less differentiation, is the fact that only a minority of men are full-time cultivators, most having some traditional or 'modern' occupation besides farming. In the sample of thirty households in Kangabusharo/Lugaze, only six of the twenty husbands were full-time farmers. Six women were managing their households and farms alone with no male family members. As will be shown later, although their workload was heavy, it was they who had the most time to give to communal work, their time being saved from serving men and taking orders from them. Both the dependent and independent women took care of children and also had the benefits of child labour. Several of the thirty households in the Bugabo village were being managed by women, some using Nyarwanda and Burundi migrant labour.

The work that only women can do was clearly specified, but most work classified as men's work could, in their absence, also be done by women. (The migrant labourers, however, could be given work otherwise belonging to women.)

The women had a very tight schedule. Although the work pattern had local variations in different parts of the District, and also according to the dry and wet seasons, both were busy. The woman's work was to

1. wake up early to prepare breakfast; clean the house;
2. prepare noon and evening meals;
3. cut grass to be laid on the floor for sitting, and remove the old grass, weekly or when necessary;
4. hoe and weed the farm, as often as every three months;
5. plant crops like beans and maize once or twice in a year. Neighbours and close friends help each other, planting one farm after another;
6. cultivate *misiri* with bambara-nuts or groundnuts, yams and potatoes, outside the village area. Nuts are cultivated once a year and the potatoes depend on the woman's time and strength and the need in the family. The *misiri* cultivation may be done two or three times a year, on two or three separate plots.

The women were busy all the year round. They rested from their agricultural work on Sundays if they were Christians, or on any holiday if they felt they could afford to rest. If there was a death in the village, nobody cultivated or weeded the fields for four days, which gave the women a break. They then busied themselves with the deceased's family, helping where needed, but generally this was a time off from work. Otherwise it depended on the individual when she felt that she did not have much to do and could rest. Older girls who were not at school were almost as busy as their mothers.

Apart from coffee and plantains, which most Haya farmers culti-vated, the other crops varied according to labour and other resources available. Tea had been introduced as a new crop, and farmers and ujamaa villagers in the neighbourhood of the tea-processing plants had been encouraged to grow it. Since tea requires regular attention, only farmers whose pattern of cultivation could accommodate extra labour demands had planted it. In our Kangabusharo/Lugaze sample, 7 out of 18 private farms had indi-vidual plots of tea, and the ujamaa village had a communal tea farm. Work on tea was done by men and women.

It appears from Priscilla Reining's analysis of the Haya farming economy in the first part of the 1950s that the women's workload was considerably lighter then than it is now. Reining has since pointed out that by the late 1960s the open land cultivation had greatly increased and many more food crops were grown than previ-ously. Since the food crops have been the women's domain, this has meant more work for women. Twenty years ago the pattern had been established whereby the man took the coffee money in order to take care of the development and management of the farm, payment of school fees and purchases of clothes, while the provision of food for the family was left to the woman. But to feed a family and provide other household necessities, the demand for which has grown with the increased necessity for consumer goods, is much more of a strain today than it was twenty years ago. The more a woman earns, the more family provisions are left for her to take care of. A man commonly takes a disproportionate part of the cash income for his own use, continuing to consider it his right to manage all the cash, whether or not he lives in the village or on the farm. At the time of the coffee harvest even an absent husband turns up to collect this money, or the wife has to put it aside for him. A common reason for divorce is the man not using the cash income for the necessities of the family.

In reality, much of the farm management in the villages is in the hands of the women. *If they had access to the income from their work and a right to regulate their own time, rapid intensification and expansion of agriculture would result.* The women are trained by daily necessity and strain to provide every family member with food and other necessities, to forgo their own pleasures and to work hard for the benefit of others. The contribution of women towards the educational support of family members has been substantial even when they have had to work against many odds. Given greater means to work with, their accomplishments would increase proportionately. The fact that independent women's farms and businesses often flourish if they have had a little initial capital is evidence of this. Yet they have all started without the man's privilege of an inherited plot of developed land and a house.

In some ujamaa villages and on larger farms, use of a tractor has facilitated diversification of crops, relieving women of the extensive time otherwise used for hoeing. Since work is plentiful, and extension of cultivation in terms of intensity, quantity and diversification is possible in Haya villages, mechanisation will not in the near future push women to the margins of agricultural production, a possibility suggested by Boserup (1970).

The woman's daily schedule keeps her busy from morning till evening with a sum total of seemingly insignificant small domestic duties. The pressure is made greater by the demands of the husband or father who expects constant readiness on the part of women to fulfil his wishes and needs. One example of this is the fact that, in accordance with tradition, a wife has to prepare food for her husband for each meal whether he comes home or not, and she is not supposed to eat from that food until the husband comes, whether that takes the whole day or even two. If she has children for whom to cook she does that separately from the husband's food and she is then likely to eat from the children's food what is left over. There are households in which this pattern is no longer followed, but such demands of double work in food preparation are still common. The right to demand the services of a wife at his will, and the duty to punish her physically, even by severe beating, is approved as belonging to the husband's authoritative role as the head of the household.

Men can easily excuse themselves from the numerous small chores left to women to do, since they consider that they are concerned with matters of greater significance. A village woman expressed her satisfaction at the thought that women were these days getting jobs in offices. 'Men have long enough excused themselves from all other work under the cover of having "office work".' Traditionally, the Haya man had the duty of daily greeting the *Mukama*, the hereditary ruler, or his representative in the neighbourhood, as well as meeting his male neighbours over some locally brewed beer to exchange daily news (Reining, *ibid.*, 48). It is from this pattern that men have been able to transfer their interests and time to political and business activities, whereas the daily necessity of all women's duties keeps them from participation. Since adult education has been made more or less compulsory, women often welcome it, considering it a holiday from their heavy work. They had the same attitude towards being interviewed for our research.

In wealthier households, women's labour can be supplemented by hired labour. This was also the case in the villages studied, where several families employed Nyarwanda immigrant labourers. Some of the labourers stayed in the villages ready to be hired by anybody offering work. They were all men, at times accompanied by their wives or relatives. The immigrant labourers could even be paid with food, which made it possible for many to hire them from time to time to supplement the women's work on the fields. In 1974 the government passed an order that everybody should cultivate a potato or cassava field, but quite a few of the men employed immigrant labourers in their stead or had their wives cultivate both plots.

On the whole the men, apart from those workers who had full-time wage employment, had a comparatively light schedule. Even if a man did manual labour somewhere or worked on his house, there were times when he had little or nothing to do and so had time to rest. In any case he regulated his own time. Even a hired labourer had more time to pause than women who managed both field and household work and attended to children.

The husband may have two farms, with a wife on each, in a single village or in two neighbouring ones. He controls them and collects the income from them. His wives, alone or with the help of some paid labour, do all the farm work and domestic duties, but they are fully dependent on the husband's goodwill for their necessities, beyond what food crops they themselves can grow. Thus one can argue that a woman's position, her share of production, the strain she faces in terms of labour input, and the benefits from her labour are not always in direct proportion to the wealth of the husband and the size and bearing capacity of his farm holdings. Of course, where the benefits are shared between husband and wife the differences between the poor peasant woman and the rich farmer's wife are striking.

On the basis of her valuable studies made in the 1950s, Reining categorically states that 'a Haya woman can never be the head of the family'. She by-passes the problem of women's general inability to inherit land by using the term 'person in charge' also for women who might have been in charge of the farms they cultivated. The data of the present study show that women who have purchased the right to the land they cultivate, or who are cultivating their own plots in ujamaa villages, are now accepted as heads of household and as holding the tenure to the plots of land they have themselves purchased. This in itself has changed the image of the woman as always being a dependant of some male members of her family, and has no doubt also encouraged other women to seek independent means of living.

When the Haya Council forbade the sale of land to returning prostitutes (see pp. 52, 77), it perhaps rightly understood that the ownership of land would encourage independent attitudes among the women and would potentially accelerate divorce rates and the women's flight to the towns. But neither the Council nor the Haya society as such felt compelled to have a look at the root issue of the problem: the discrimination against women which made them servants and dependants. Women have not been allowed to inherit, nor to have any permanent share in the wealth they accrued through their work, nor to be consulted in transactions concerning family wealth. The woman has been in the position of an inferior for whom, like a child, decisions have been made by her male protectors, and who has been rewarded and punished at their discretion.

At present, the majority of peasant women continue in this position. At the same time, there are enough individual cases of women who have broken off from this male tutelage to cause a considerable gulf between these two categories of women. Married women often look askance at independent women in the villages as well as in the towns, and experience them as a threat, although they are also envious of their greater freedom. Since the image of the independent woman has carried with it the connotation of semi-prostitution, it is not an easy task for such a woman to establish a position of respectability. She can, however, be given political leadership positions, and her contribution to her local society can be recognised when she financially supports her children and relatives and offers her labour in village development. In the Bugabo village one of the two female members on the Marriage Conciliation Board (cf. note 7, p. 121 below) was a former prostitute from the big cities of Kenya, who was now held up by the village elders as an exemplary member of village society, living on her own, supporting the children of friends and managing her farm.

The presence of determined, independent women in the villages is a clear indication that the present reality no longer corresponds to the recognised ideology of the traditionally-based society. This means that the expressed social and economic goals of the society need to be brought into line with present-day reality. The political ideology of greater equality between the sexes is in fact not a completely alien concept but already corresponds to certain developments in society. Full realisation of the changed conditions and of women's responses to these changes will help Haya society to re-examine and re-state its ideology in terms of the country's policy concerning women.

Village ujamaa development

The villagisation programme in Bukoba District has mainly affected people with little or no land, or people living in remote areas who have been moved to places closer to the existing roads. The data for this study are insufficient to draw any general conclusions about the effects of ujamaa development on the women. The intention is rather to compare the possibilities that village development offers for women with their traditional pattern of life. The realisation of this potential even in the best villages is an accomplishment still awaited, but an awareness of the problems and of the resources of women at the stage of village formation is likely to be of assistance in the ongoing development process.

The terms 'villagisation' and 'village development' are used here for the country-wide restructuring of the rural areas, whereby the total rural population were brought to live in planned villages (see Chapter 1, pp. 12–13). At present such villages are either reorga-nised traditional ones or newly-established villages where people have moved from the surrounding areas for the enhancement of their own development. Only a few such villages have so far devel-oped as actual ujamaa villages, with substantial communal cultiva-tion and cooperative activities. At best, villages at this stage are so-called cooperative villages. However, many which started with the intention of becoming ujamaa villages call themselves so even when the full ujamaa stage has not been reached. This is the case with those used as case material here, Kangabusharo, a reorganised village, and Kilimelile, a newly-established village.

Kangabusharo communal activities

The work pattern in Kangabusharo ujamaa village differed from that in the traditional villages, in that communal work was done three mornings a week in addition to the work on individual fields. Both men and women were involved in the work. The communal activities were:

Agriculture. Tea-growing, started in June 1970. In April 1974 there were 18 acres of tea, in June 1975 12 acres. This brought in some income to the village all the time, but the people themselves were paid only a shilling a day for their labour. The women had a communal sweet potato farm.

Carpentry cooperative. Started in 1970, it had a reasonable balance by February 1974.

Small brick-making cooperative. Also started in 1970 to help young men, but due to rains it had run at a loss.

Ujamaa shop. Started in November 1971 from the assets of other projects. It stocked some basic necessities.

UWT (women's organisation). Made and sold handicrafts, table cloths, children's clothes etc.[4]

When the Kangabusharo communal tea-growing began in 1970, men organised it and joined in larger numbers than women; only four out of 24 founding members were women. By April 1974 the number of registered men was 21, while 27 women had become active members. When the first distribution of income was made according to labour input, 21 out of 35 receiving payment were women. In the second distribution, 19 out of 32 were women. At the third distribution women received a total of 212 shillings, while men got 196 shillings. Five youths were learning carpentry and had formed their own small cooperative, as had those who were making bricks. But women also had other cooperative activities in UWT, and cultivated annual crops through a mutual-aid group, *kyama*. The women's *kyama* had been formed fourteen years earlier, as an extension of a similar men's organisation. The members of the *kyama* were older women. They spent their time in turn on each other's fields, doing the complete cultivation of one woman's land in one day. The harvesting was done in the same manner. They also helped each other in family celebrations and gave special contributions of money and work when any member was ill or in special need, or when a family member had died. Such a *kyama* seemed to have offered a more natural use of cooperation than the officially-organised UWT, which on the whole was started from outside as something extra, instead of incorporating into itself the existing forms of women's cooperation. The *kyama* had twenty members who at the time were not generally members of the ujamaa village.

The women living singly were more active participants in communal work and meetings than married women, although even they were taking care of children and had to manage their own work in the fields without the supposed help from men. There was ample evidence here, as elsewhere, that married women's participation in organisational and decision-making activities was often discouraged by husbands, directly or indirectly. So far, communal work had not replaced private farming; it was an additional demand on women's strength. Women who managed their own lives could organise their work and decide to devote more time to communal cultivation, while married women were tied to their daily routine of domestic service and care of the husband's fields in such a way that only through common consultation and agreement could it be changed. This kind of consultation very seldom took place, since men were used to making their decisions on their own. As things stood, women provided the larger share of communal work, but in the Village Committee they were represented by only two women out of ten committee members. (A third woman who was absent from the village most of the time was also on the committee in addition to the 10 people mentioned.)

The current leaders of women's activities had learned their organisational skills in the women's organisation of the Lutheran Church, known as Betania, which was also active in the village. All the women members of the ujamaa village were also automatically members of UWT, whether they had paid for their membership or not. They were also all members of TANU. UWT had its own fund and operated in three ways. Members had their cooperative potato field on which they worked on Thursdays, while they were supposed to work on the communal tea farm on Mondays, Tuesdays and Saturdays. UWT members also provided labour assistance to each other in preparing fields, or they helped needy members. The third form of activity had been sewing items for sale.

The UWT had been run under the supervision of men through the Village Committee until April 1974, after which time the women were allowed by the committee to start their own fund. The decision was made to start selling fish. The resistance which this effort met on the part of men, not least because it would mean an overnight stay away from home, discouraged several women. However, the business was started.

In order to facilitate the women's work, the village had started a day care centre. This also took children from surrounding villages. At one time there had been 45 children enrolled; in June 1975 there were 15 children, as the older ones had moved on to primary school.

While the women recognised the usefulness of pre-school education for the smaller children, they also felt that the day care centre as it operated, taking in only children above 4 years of age (or occasionally 3 years) for a few hours in the morning, was not always a help to the mother, because those very children were needed at home to look after the smallest ones. Yet to organise a day care centre for younger children was beyond the capacity of the village.

Kilimelile

Another ujamaa village in Bukoba District, Kilimelile, had received publicity especially in regard to the role of women in ujamaa development, as it was at the time the only one in the country with a woman in the chair. Hamisa Amani had been active in TANU in Bukoba town and had been elected as a local vice chairperson. When the call for ujamaa village development was put out in 1968, she decided to go to a village to be established in Kilimelile and to start cultivating. Other women from Bukoba followed her example, and eventually, according to the Chairwoman's estimate, half of the 250 households in the village had a woman as the head. To start the new life had not been easy, but the initial difficulties had been overcome. In discussing with researchers the reasons why women wanted to make themselves independent, the women said, 'You know how the men oppress us' ('*Unajua wanaume wanavyotutesa*').

The total Kilimelile village population was given as 838, although figures fluctuated because some people had left in search of employment. The village counted 165 working members in June 1975, many of whom had come from great distances, and represented several ethnic backgrounds: Haya, Ha, Rwanda and others. Each had a plot of 1 or 2 acres, which was cultivated individually. The village had set aside some 3,000 acres of land for future development. Communal cultivation of beans was started in 1972, and brought a good income that year. In the following year, wild pigs destroyed the communal fields and nothing was sold. In 1974, 25 acres were cultivated and from this the initial capital for opening a cooperative shop was obtained. There was a good harvest in 1975, but most of the beans were cultivated and sold on an individual basis. Four large lorryloads of beans had already been sold at the time of the study. The villagers were hoping to get a tractor to enable them to cultivate larger areas and also to cultivate maize and rice communally. The days set aside for communal work, for five morning hours, were Monday, Wednesday and Saturday. Water was a major problem, and was being transported into the village by army lorries.

The village had organised two study groups for the beginning of a radio adult education campaign, using the two radios they owned, one for the village and the other in school. So far the primary school had three standards, and two teachers ran six adult education points.

Hamisa Amani became the Chairwoman in 1972. One of her

accomplishments had been to settle as members of the village a number of immigrant labourers from Ngara and Rwanda who had been working for pay on other farmers' fields. She felt there was a degree of opposition from men who wanted to keep their wives under their rule. They had on occasion blamed her for creating disobedience from the wives through the women's meetings. But in her opinion both men and women had in general accepted her leadership. The Chairwoman's view can be contrasted with that presented in Zinnat Bader's study of Kilimelile village (1975, 33). The writer shows that this woman leader had sided with the wealthier men in giving favours to certain factions in the village, thus encouraging economic inequality. Bader brings out evidence in other cases too that class solidarity is stronger than female solidarity, the latter working mainly along class lines.

Since women have seldom owned anything individually, it is much easier for them to think in terms of common ownership. They have also been accustomed to share in work, both in domestic duties at any family festival, ritual occasion or in times of mourning, and in taking turns on each other's fields to lighten another woman's load. Thus the promotion of communal cultivation among women is no more difficult than getting women working on roads or other such village enterprises. The principal obstacle is the fact that women continue to be under the rule of their husbands, whose resistance towards communal work stems partly from their reluctance to see their wives participate in it.

The fact that women can be registered as independent members of a village and receive returns for their own work, as is the case on the tea farm, where each worker gets an equal share according to his or her hours of work, is most beneficial from the viewpoint of the women.

Women's economic position in relation to marital status

The status of a person's clan is a factor within social relationships influencing decisions even in the modern sector, although no overt recognition is given to it these days. However, when the *nyarubanja* tenant system was abolished, the loss of land for the former landowners meant, at least in some cases, a loss of status because of their inability to work their own farms. How widely this was the case could not be ascertained within this research.

The wealth of a family is no longer directly related to clan background. Education, which was largely provided by the Catholic and Lutheran Churches, opened up opportunities for all levels of society. In fact it is said here, as on the Coast, that a man belonging to the ruling dynasty sometimes sent a serf's child to school rather than his own. Although the first educational attempts may have been directed especially towards the chief's descendants, the modernisation trend which gathered up the young males soon became a more general phenomenon. Education here, as elsewhere, has resulted in its recipients earning salaries from which they have made financial or other contributions to their families, and this has facilitated increased cash crop production and has accelerated trade. More recently, the fact that with the disestablishment of the *nyarubanja* system a former landowner could be left with a plot of land no larger than that of his former tenants, and with little practice in working it, has divorced the economic status from the social one. At present the social status scale commonly has an economic base independent of clan status. However, in individual cases in which educational, economic and inherited clan positions coincide, the class status of such a person is fairly well defined.

The change from an economic base linked with inherited social status, to one in which status depends on one's education and entre-preneurial successes in cash crop production and trade, has not changed the peasant woman's position. In both, the woman has remained economically weak. Her status as the wife of a wealthy man is socially higher than as the wife of an impoverished one, whatever the former status of her clan. However, the day she is divorced, she is left in either case with little or nothing, and even while living with the husband she may be deprived of any chance of earning income or of being adequately supported for family needs.

The evidence from individual family histories in sample villages reveals a lack of essential personal commodities, such as clothes and nutritious food items, among the wives of both poor and wealthier men. On the other hand, there are cases where more equal sharing has resulted in the freer use of cash for personal effects among wealthier farmers' wives.

Zinnat Bader's study indicates that class differences become apparent in women's attendance at communal activities and in their differentiated patterns of cooperation. She also found some wealthier women in Kikukwe village who owned inherited land. The present evidence does not permit statistically-supported general-isations, but the case studies of women in the samples of this study point to the fact that the married woman's position is conspicuously vulnerable.

Position of widows

One of the basic direct causes which have pushed women off the land to live in towns is the fact that wives and female descendants

have not as a rule been able to inherit immovable property, especially land. According to customary law, land to which a clan has
rights cannot be transferred to a woman.[5] A widow may be a
guardian of a male heir and have charge over the plantation and
house until the son grows up. She shares this responsibility with a
male co-guardian from the husband's family. A daughter can only
be given a piece of land to cultivate by the father if land is available,
and while she is alive she can deal with it as if it were hers, but her
descendants cannot inherit it and she cannot sell it; it returns to her
father's descendants. A widow who had a son could not remarry,
according to the old custom. In 1946 this was changed through a rule
made by the Council of Chiefs whereby 'the widow of a marriage by
native custom is . . . free and eligible for remarrying either within or
outside her late husband's clan, as she may choose' (Gustafsson,
1972, 44; Philips, 1953, 209). Before that, the widow could only be
taken as a wife by the husband's brother, as has commonly been the
custom in patrilineal societies (levirate).

The difficulties for a widow occur particularly if she does not
have a male child or does not have any children at all. According to
custom, a woman inherited by the husband's brother could be sent
away by him, and the brother could then claim the original
bridewealth back from her father. Should the widow later give
birth to a son, no matter how much time had elapsed, the son
would be considered to belong to the former husband, whose heir
he would become (a *bisisi* child — see p. 72). A widow had, and
still has, the option of returning to her father's plantation. Her
share in the land in most cases is only a small plot in the neighbourhood of her father's or her brother's house, a situation in
which she is made to feel her inferiority and dependence on her
brothers or their descendants. Social ostracism accompanies the
economic inferiority.

Case studies were made of thirteen women who were staying near
their brothers' houses in a Bugabo village. In one or two rare cases
the woman had inherited the right to her father's plot of land, but
she could only really call it her own in a case where in the whole
family line there were no male heirs to the deceased father, either in
his own or in his brother's family.

Of the women living near or in their brother's houses only one was
a widow. She was 55 years old, and had been picked up by the chief's
men from her village 45 years earlier to be a servant girl (*muzana*) in
the chief's court, later being given by him as a present to a friend
with whom she lived as one of several wives. She never bore a child
and after the death of her husband she left the husband's household
because she felt despised by her in-laws, who had never accepted her

as an equal because of her lower social origin. She had returned to her original village and was living in her brother's house at the time of the study, fully participating in work and caring for the brother's property.

In an area of 30 houses surveyed in the same village, several houses were occupied by widows, some continuing to live on the farms which they had built up together with their husbands. Two of these had no children. In both cases the husband and wife belonged to the Revival Movement, *balokole*, and the husbands had remained faithful to their wives and died without heirs. One of these men had ordered his brother to let his wife continue to live on their farm or else to compensate her fully if he took the house and the land as his rightful inheritance. Since the brother was working and living in Dar es Salaam, he was letting the widow live on and benefit from the land until she died. In the other case the widow was already old, and the house and farm had no male heir. So if a widow can inherit her husband's house and farm and benefit from it, there must be a very special set of circumstances to allow it.

In the sample of 30 women in Lugaze and Kangabusharo villages, five were widows. Three of these had sons and thus continued to live on their husband's land. One had only two girls, and she too was living next to the husband's relatives with the second daughter, while the first had left for town. The remaining widow had left for town after the husband died at an early stage of their marriage, because the plot of land allotted to her was insufficient to support her. She had made enough money as a prostitute to manage to buy a field on her return, and she later joined the ujamaa village. Although at present a man can sell his land without asking the consent of anyone who is not a direct heir, it cannot yet be conceived of that a father would have the right to allocate a piece of land to his daughters which she would be able to pass on to her children.

One Bugabo man who had begotten only two female children, and from Christian principles did not want to take a second wife, before his death allocated his land to his wife and his second daughter, who was barren and consequently had been divorced. This right was disputed by the dead man's brother. The women were helped by the husband of the first daughter to take the matter to court and, through a court decision, they were given the right of occupancy for life. However, their right to dispose of the land is not recognised, although if they were men they would have that right. The 500–700 shillings a man may get from his land when selling it to an outsider is for him more important than his sister's or daughter's welfare, although the woman could in a year or two produce crops worth more than that.

The mere idea that a woman should be given land in her own right was still foreign at the time of the research, although the number of women who had purchased land for themselves with their own money was growing. Their right to the land for which they have paid is not tied to the traditional system of inheritance and is thus their individual right. But a woman who has been left alone to get the initial capital for establishing herself as a farmer has to find some means of earning that money, and in order to do this, large numbers of Haya women have taken the road of prostitution, selling the only thing they are left with.

Divorce

The Haya marriage arrangement had less emphasis as a union between clans than, for example, in Chagga society, unless it was between high-status families. The wife's family had no rights in the children of their daughter, and could not look forward to any benefits from her marriage. This may be related to the fact that when a man married a woman from a clan below his own in status, his children naturally had to remain in his clan so as not to be lowered in status. Unequal clan status and the fact that chiefs and landowners used their right to tribute as a means of obtaining wives and concubines may also have influenced the marriage system as such, de-emphasising clan linkages through marriage. This in turn facilitated divorce.

Divorce in Haya language is expressed by the term 'driving away', *kutambya*, which in itself gives an indication of what the main form of divorce has been. On the other hand, there are also many accounts of wives having left their husbands and children, having been aggrieved by something, or just looking for better opportunities. The man's right to divorce his wife was recognized in the traditional system, and he could not be forced to keep a wife he did not want. The father accepted this fact, as well as his duty to pay back the bridewealth. Since every father of daughters knew that he might be faced with having to return the bridewealth, this may account for the payments being generally fairly low compared with many other ethnic groups (Cory and Hartnoll, 1945, 59), although in clans of equal status the father could demand larger sums of compensation as the bridegroom's 'feeding money' during his visits to the bride's house before marriage. This could amount to considerable sums, and was not repayable.

According to Haya custom, if a wife runs into a problem with her husband, she can return to her father's house. The husband is then supposed to come and take the matter up with the father, who calls together a clan council of elders to evaluate the situation (*kutahya* — to apologise). The guilty party has to provide compensation, usually a goat and beer, to reconcile the matter. If the husband wants to divorce his wife, he can beat her until she runs away. If he does not follow her to her father's house to settle the quarrel, her departure is counted as final and it is considered a divorce. Nowadays the council of elders is often replaced by a Marriage Conciliation Board, or the persons concerned may prefer a council of more private composition.

Rehse, describing the northern Haya, Kiziba, marriage early in the twentieth century, stressed that there was an affectionate relationship between individual family members ('The man loves his wife and she loves him'), a fact which Bishop Kibira confirms (Rehse, 1910, 93; Kibira, 1974, 29–30). Kibira also refers to the countless folk–songs connected with love and lovers, as well as the custom of sending presents to each other during courtship. One assumes that where there is emphasis on the relationship between individuals, the chance of a marriage becoming dissolved would be greater than if the arrangement were made between families and clans. A marriage which started as a social and economic arrangement would continue as such, while a relationship between individuals would be freer from external enforcements, more liable to be affected by individual feelings and consequently more easily broken up. According to Rehse and Kibira, even traditionally the man made his own choice first and then informed his parents about it (*ibid.*).

Divorce has been a common occurrence in Haya marriage over a long period. A group of 100 teachers writing their autobiographies in 1943–4 considered it a special privilege if their mothers were living with them (Sundkler, 1974). Polygyny was common, and unwillingness to accept a position as one of many wives made women prefer to leave their husbands.

The frequency of divorces is borne out by the sample of 30 families referred to earlier. In these immediate families, 40 divorces of wives and daughters had occurred (34 wives, 5 daughters, one daughter-in-law). Of the divorced women 8 were known to have gone into prostitution, 7 permanently, one temporarily. The reasons for divorce were given in 23 cases; among these, one husband had divorced 10 times and another 5 times. Reasons given for divorce were the husband's non-support of the family (in 14 cases, including the men with several divorces), the husband's cruelty (2 cases), no children (4 cases), the attraction of better opportunities in town life (one case) and an accusation of witchcraft (2 cases). In 2 other cases it was specified that the husband chased his wife away. Where the husband's support was stated to be inadequate, the husband had taken the coffee money and all the income from the farm, but had not in return supported the wife and family. In the Bugabo village of R., in an area of 20 households, 26 divorces were recorded in the immediate families.

In R. and B. villages, 15 women were interviewed who had been away from the village practising prostitution. The circumstantial or stated reasons for prostitution revealed that in 8 cases the women had left the village because they had had no children and their husbands had married other wives. Four had only female children, with similar consequences. The remaining three had problems with brothers and their own family after divorce.

The rate for divorced women above 15 years of age in the Kagera (West Lake) Region in the 1967 census was 10%, whereas in the Kilimanjaro Region, for example, it was 2.7%. Even for women in the Coast Region divorces are frequent, the figure being 7.9% (excluding Dar es Salaam). The corresponding figures in the 1978 census were 8% (9.8% for urban, 6.1% for rural) in Kagera; 3.8% (4.8% urban, 2.8% rural) in Kilimanjaro, and 10% in the Coast Region (12.1% urban, 7.9% rural).

Although children are by custom not allowed to stay with their divorced mothers, the latter often show remarkable concern and care for them, even in cases when they are hardly allowed to see them. Examples can be quoted of prostitutes who have taken up that life in order to provide their children with education. Other examples give evidence of hard-working divorced women who, with a minimal initial sum of money, have purchased a small plot of land and through that and through additional income from casual labour have paid for their children's education and provided them with clothes. A divorced woman in Bugabo, who had been forbidden to see her son because she had taken the husband to court, had continued to work so that the son could get an education. A divorced woman in Bukoba town was living, most reluctantly, as the mistress of a married man, and trading during the day-time, in order to support not only her children but her mother and a 'good-for-nothing' brother in her home village in Bugabo. Yet the brother was holding the inherited land and had been given the opportunity for continued education in place of the capable sister who had desired to have the education.

'Bisisi' children

Related to the frequent divorces is the *bisisi* system in many parts of Bukoba District. Under the system a man who is the first to have intercourse with an unmarried girl, or who after any childbirth is the first to have intercourse — symbolic or real — with the woman, is considered to be the father of the first child born after this incident. In this way a man can secure children for himself, no matter what his marital circumstances are. If divorce takes place children cannot as a rule, according to custom, stay with their mothers.

In the Kangabusharo/Lugaze sample the husband had kept the children in 11 cases. (The husband with 10 divorced wives and another with 5 have been here counted as one case each.) The 10-times-divorced man had 9 children from previous marriages living with him, several of whom were *bisisi* children. One of the mothers was nursing a child which would be sent to the husband after weaning. The man who had divorced 5 wives was at the same time living with a wife with no children (she had been divorced before by another husband because of barrenness). The childless wife was taking care of 5 *bisisi* children from previous wives. This shows how even a sterile man can, following the *bisisi* system, be provided with male heirs. *Bisisi* children cannot inherit if there is a male child born of a normal marriage, but if the man does not have such a male child the *bisisi* child becomes the heir. While the *bisisi* system assures men of children, it robs women even of those they have while they are single. At the same time, it offers support for otherwise fatherless children. It can happen that the fatherhood of *bisisi* children is only formally recognised, while the children remain in the custody of the mothers. Such children can be brought to their fathers as fully-grown adults, as with two *bisisi* children in Bugabo. One of them came to his father at 30 years of age.

The *bisisi* system is kept alive through sanctions relating to the spirit world. Cases were narrated in Bugabo in which neglecting to bring the *bisisi* child to the father was believed to bring about the anger of the ancestors and cause the death of other children in the family.

There is evidence that taking a *bisisi* child at an early age to the supposed father, with whom the mother has had nothing to do for years, may cause the child to feel unwanted and result in behaviour disturbances. The father himself may not be interested in the child, or his wife or wives may resent the child's presence. Two of the returned prostitutes in Bugabo had been unwanted *bisisi* children.

Prostitution

We have seen that the choices left for divorced women and widows with no male children are very few, and the support offered to them in the form of a small plot of land in a position of dependence on male relatives is not always acceptable. Neither is it sufficient or satisfying for the women concerned. It is particularly inadequate in cases where the woman is determined to help her children to get better living conditions and education and to give support to her mother, who may be left in a position of need similar to her own. The road of prostitution has been opened for the Haya women in the past, and it is known to have brought worthwhile returns to many who have chosen it. Many Haya women launch on such a career with hopes of establishing themselves as economically independent women.

The fifteen former prostitutes interviewed in two Bugabo villages had spent an average of 7 years in various East African towns practising prostitution. The towns specified by ten women were Mombasa, Kisumu, Nairobi, Tororo, Kampala, Tanga, Mwanza and Dar es Salaam.

That the desire for economic independence is strong among the young women of today became evident from the answers to questions put to Standard 7 leavers in a Home Craft School about their future plans. They hoped to get work in order to develop themselves, to have an income and to be able to serve their fellow-women. The university students working on the Haya study concluded from their investigations that the principal factor driving women to prostitution is not poverty but rather the independent spirit of Haya women, who do not want to subject themselves to the kind of master-servant relationship they often meet in marriage.

It has been argued that because the Haya women have a sense of independence they could have established themselves in trade instead of going into prostitution, since even their prostitution is said to be of a highly commercialised kind (Southall and Gutkind, 1957, 82). The basic reasons are considered by some researchers to be psychological and are looked for in a woman's irregular family background. The same kind of argument is put forward by Carlebach about juvenile prostitution in Nairobi (Gustafsson, 1972, 53ff).

Obviously the unstable home situation, with children often being separated from their mothers, must be a significant factor also in Haya country, but in itself it is a symptom rather than a cause. In the village samples we can find some evidence that a precedent established by other women relatives, often the mother, pushes daughters into prostitution.

In ten of the thirty families in Kangabusharo/Lugaze, a wife, a daughter or an aunt had been or was a prostitute. Two of the practising young prostitutes in the village sample were daughters of a prostitute mother who had deserted her 9 children and was living in Dar es Salaam. One woman who later returned to her husband had gone to Mombasa with her aunt, who was a prostitute. She also gave as a common reason why women go the fact that a mother or a close relative encouraged them to follow in her footsteps. Even if there are no such precedents of prostitution in the family, the fact that children stay with the father after a divorce means that they are taken care of by women other than their own mother. When *bisisi* children were studied in a Bugabo village, 4 out of 10 had a history of some kind of disturbance and ostracism. Those with difficulties had been taken to their supposed fathers' households as children. Thus poor home background perpetuates the problem of women and leads them to look for solutions through channels which the preceding generations have opened. However, the basic women's problem cannot be separated from its economic premises.

The historical roots of prostitution have already been traced to the fact that women were in the past treated as commodities of exchange. The causes inherent in the economic and social structure of the society have also been briefly referred to. There is also evidence that some Haya fathers have in fact, for economic reasons, encouraged Haya prostitution. Data collected on town women indicated that money-earning women are often faithful supporters of their rural relatives. The opinion is held by older women that they are better supported by their daughters than their sons, if the former are in a position to give such support. This fact may be presented in support of the opinion that prostitution has been backed by fathers' encouragement of their daughters' money-earning activities in town, of whatever nature.

In the Kiongozi newspaper during 1961, there was a debate between some Haya fathers about whether Haya parents encouraged prostitution or not.[6] A father wrote a description of the way in which fathers made use of their daughters and did not try to persuade them to remain with their husbands if they indicated a desire to run away from them. 'To speak the truth, it is a fact known by all Tanganyikans that Haya parents should be strongly blamed for the increase in prostitution in Buhaya[7]. . . . Prostitution in Buhaya is a matter which the parents of prostitutes have welcomed and nurtured quite openly.' The process was described in the article as follows. A daughter who has run into a quarrel with her husband goes to her parents to complain about him. Without listening to the other side of the story, the parents advise the girl to run away from her husband and to go to some town. Parents are even found secretly seeing the girl off to the steamer having given her the fare. After a while the girl writes back to her parents, sending them money equivalent to the bridewealth that her husband had paid for her (a sum which is not generally large). The husband, who has been wondering about his wife's whereabouts, is informed about her and the money is returned to him. When the girl later comes to visit her parents they are waiting for her at the port, and she returns with clothes and gifts for them.

The students conducting the village study also gave evidence that fathers were partly to blame for women leaving the villages. It had also been observed by Sundkler, in 1943–4, that women returned with bicycles and gifts of clothing for their waiting relatives (Sundkler, 1947). The Haya women in towns have kept an air of respectability by engaging in commercial activities during the day and being good tenants, keeping up their rent payments regularly (Perkin, 1969, 288; Leslie, 1957). This also made it easier for their rural relatives to preserve an image of respectability while exploiting their daughters.

Three of the ten women in the Kangabusharo/Lugaze village sample who had themselves been prostitutes in other towns had returned with sufficient money to purchase land and settle in the village. All but one of the returned prostitutes in Bugabo had established themselves in the village with land and a house.

It was observed by those doing the village study that the only village women with some economic means of their own were those who had practised prostitution. This was witnessed in the village by other women who may have tried to get a divorce in the hope of economic gain. One of these former prostitutes had a beer–brewing business, and fields which she had cultivated partly by tractor and partly by the labour of Rwandan workers. Bader's case studies (*ibid.*) bring out the fact that independent women in villages work in cooperation with the men's *kyama* and not with the *kyama* of women, a factor causing antagonism between them and married women. These women are very generally — not only in Haya country — elected as women's representatives to committees on all levels. All this enhances prostitution in the eyes of other deprived women, as something worth trying. This in turn leads to the prevalent but misconceived notion that prostitution results if women are granted greater freedom of decision and control of their own lives and means, the symptom being seen as the cause.

Towards a solution

We can tentatively draw the conclusion that prostitution has been the Haya women's response to the conditions which have too often treated the woman as an inferior being, a commodity of exchange, a tenant and a servant who could be dismissed at the will of the husband, and used for producing children who were then stolen from her. At the time of the study there had been very little official recognition in Haya society of the fact that its women were in a vulnerable position. In the past, the question of prostitution had been dealt with by negative measures, such as preventing women from leaving the area by checking the buses and boats. On one occasion when this happened, some women chartered a plane to Nairobi (Gustafsson. 1972). Other ways were to forbid them re-entry, and even refuse to sell land to prostitutes, so that there would be no inducement for an increased exodus of women hoping to return with money to become independent farmers.

There have been attempts to provide women with training in crafts and jobs which would offer them an economic base with no need to prostitute themselves. This measure of restoration also deals with the results, not the cause. If the matter is to be dealt with, it requires the reform of women's position in rural society in such a way that women, whether married or alone, will have chances equal to those enjoyed by the male members of the society to earn both subsistence and cash income from their own labour. As long as the title to land is held by individual families, ways must be found for a woman to have equal opportunity with a man to hold title to the land she cultivates. There is no reason why, if married, she should not be able to enjoy the fruits of her labour and why the husband should not bear an equal share of the toil and cost related to the care of the family. Should she be divorced, she needs sufficient land or cash to enable her to buy a piece of land for cultivation. Because land within the ujamaa system is dealt with as a communal commodity, in principle only the work put into developing the land should be evaluated and paid for, but the land itself should not be sold. Uncultivated land should be shared freely among those who are ready to work it. If this were the case, women would utilize more land and production would rise.

In the properly operating ujamaa village system the women would have their chances. This happens if the Party directive is enforced and all working people are registered as individual members of the village who have their due share of land rights and receive returns for their work on the basis of their input. However, if women's rights concerning land and inheritance are not sufficiently guarded in ujamaa villages, the women may find themselves in the same situation as in a traditional village, the husband claiming the rights to the private plots and the income therefrom. As things stood during the study, only when cash returns from the daily communal work were encouraging could the participation in ujamaa village development be helpful to married women.

NOTES

1. The first unit consisted of four Germans, 50 Swahili listed as soldiers, and 400 armed carriers (Moffett, 1958, 66).
2. This was at the time when the people who joined in cooperative activities had decided to form an ujamaa village, before the enactment of village legislation and unification of village organisation.
3. *Misiri* is cultivation outside the village areas, on plots of land which must lie fallow for several years.
4. Some figures from the communal activities are as follows. The tea harvest June 1972-March 1974 brought in 1,207 shillings. The carpentry cooperative had a balance of 1,700 shillings by February 1974. The ujamaa shop began with 683 shillings, and had assets of 1,702 shillings in April 1974. UWT had made 207 shillings by March 1974, and the village had contributed 57 shillings to it. In Kilimelile the cooperative shop had assets of 13,000 shillings in 1975. (UWT = *Umoja wa Wanawake wa Tanzania*, Women's Union of Tanzania.)
5. There was one exception to this rule: the daughters of the ruling royal clans inherited a field on the death of their father. This was possible because of the rule of *endogamy* (marriage within the clan) which, at least earlier in their history, seems to have been the practice in the royal clans.
6. Response to an article appearing 1 Feb. 1961.
7. Buhaya means 'Haya country'.

3

WOMAN AS PRODUCER AND PROVIDER IN MOSHI DISTRICT

Focus on the Chagga

The perspective of tradition

In the development of the Chagga people on the slopes of Mt Kilimanjaro there are elements which parallel those among the Haya: a concentration of population in limited fertile areas, centralised rule by chiefs with considerable power, a mixed agricultural and livestock economy with coffee as the principal cash crop, and a ready acceptance of new influences, particularly in the form of education.

Long before the occupation of the territory by Europeans, the Chagga farmers had developed an ingenious system of damming up the numerous rivers and streams for irrigation purposes, and this system is still in operation, although pressure on land has affected the balanced use of water and land.

In the past, the irrigation system contributed to a state of prosperity based on the cultivation of banana and maize (formerly millet) and cattle-keeping. Because of the social organisation necessary for the regulation of the irrigation trenches, stratification developed, with a special class of overseers (Gutmann, 1928, 512–3). At the same time, cooperative efforts were necessary for the maintenance of the waterways. In fact, cooperation in daily life came to be a commonly–cited characteristic of this ethnic group, still quoted today when the socialistic character of their life is emphasised by some leading members of Chagga society.

Christian missionaries (mainly Roman Catholic and Lutheran) found their teachings quickly accepted and encouraged by many of the leaders in the Kilimanjaro area. Motivation towards educational achievement already existed, and this then found expression in the development of scores of educational institutions. The Chagga comprise only 3.6% of the population of Tanzania, yet a much higher percentage of secondary school and university graduates in the country are of Chagga origin; 12.4% of the students attending secondary schools in 1967 were from Kilimanjaro Region.

The planting of the first coffee tree at Kilema Catholic Mission in 1918 eventually brought about a change in the agricultural pattern of the people in Kilimanjaro. Coffee-growing increased rapidly, altering the basic mode of subsistence farming to cash cropping. It is commonly said that no man is a Chagga without his cattle and his coffee. However, because of the growing population, farms have been greatly reduced in size and a number of Chagga have moved to live on the plains, where little coffee is grown (Mascarenhas and Rudengren, 1973; Maro, 1974).

In addition to the family plot (*kihamba*) of coffee and banana trees and a small vegetable garden, most families cultivate another field, *shamba*, on the plains, *pori*, usually some distance from the homestead. There maize, beans or other crops are grown and used both for their cash value and as food for the family. *Shamba* land is almost totally restricted to the lower slopes or plains and is often rented for the planting of annual crops.

With the change from food crops, such as millet, to cash crops, the ownership of land on the mountain, formerly held on a clan and lineage basis, had to be more clearly defined. Even before the introduction of cash crops, a unilineal inheritance system had developed to ensure that the land did not pass from one clan to another and thus endanger territorial security. The land passed from the father to the eldest and youngest sons as the prime inheritors, and to the father's brothers or their inheritors as secondary heirs if the father had no sons.

With the development of a cash economy ownership has been more and more narrowed down to the individual family. The youngest son has the duty and privilege of taking over the homestead and the surrounding fields, whereas the eldest son inherits a part of the outer fields. A father with sufficient means also provides his other sons with plots of land he has usually purchased elsewhere. The result has been the division of land into such small holdings that part of the population has become impoverished.

A consequence of the individualisation of land ownership has been that it has become imperative for a man to have a son as heir. This forces a man with only daughters, as well as a man with no children, to look for another wife. Thus the unilineal inheritance system has carried over into the individual ownership system regardless of the fact that clan ownership is no longer valid. No transfer of land may pass from the father to his daughter and on to her children, but must pass via sons. There are, however, exceptions to the general rule.

Since the Law of Marriage Act (1971) recognises separate property rights for the marriage partners, there would be no danger that the husband of the daughter would take over the property and pass it on to other members of his lineage if the rights of the daughter's children were specified at the time of dividing the estate. However, ambiguity in the interpretation of the customary laws and its application to the present situation leaves open the possibility that an old customary practice might at a crucial point overrule the intended arrangement. Thus inheritance customs continue as if they related to the days of clan or lineage ownership of land.

There is such a strong sense of the rightness of the patrilineal inheritance system among the Chagga that the possibility that children of a father from another lineage or clan would inherit would seem to mean that another lineage and so also another clan would in fact be taking the land, since children get their clanship through their father. Yet an individual could sell the land with no feeling of regret on the part of clan members. In other words, individual ownership exists in terms of individual economic benefits, but the social connotations remain in the traditional framework of clan ownership. Each of these aspects reinforces the other, making the woman powerless. Her only recourse is to gain sufficient economic power herself to be able to compete in terms of ownership by purchasing land which cannot be alienated from her and which she can pass on to whom ever she wants without depending on any other family member. Thus a woman's property, when acquired with her own earnings, is in a real sense individual property, not tied to the regulations of the lineage or any kin.

If a woman in an exceptional case inherits a piece of land from her father, as may happen when a father is especially fond of his daughter, and the father does not have a male inheritor, she may lose her right to that piece at the time of dividing the estate for various customary regulations. A case in which the father separated a small plot for his own burial–place serves as an example of the foresight of a father who intended that his land should remain the property of his daughter. Had he not done this, and if he had been buried on the daughter's share of land, the whole plot could have have been claimed later by some male members of the family on account of it being the family's burial-ground and thus lineage land (Inf. by K. Makundi).

The social system of the Chagga society has offered an excellent structural setting for a man to exercise his authority. It has offered him a base from which he has formulated an ideological rationale for the superiority of male roles over female roles. Although traditional aspects are minimised in other areas of life, man's control and superiority are continually emphasised through the devices that the traditional patrilineal social system offers.

The teaching given to Chagga youth (Gutmann, 1933) shows that in the past the young men were reminded that they were not *alone* responsible for the birth of a child, that the woman had her part in it too. It would seem that this reminder was necessary because there was an over-emphasis on the man's part in the conception of a child and on the hereditary traits that come from the father. After birth, the paternal grandfather had to find some signs in the child which would clearly indicate that the child belonged to his family. Otherwise the child could not be accepted as an offspring of the father's family.

In traditional initiation rites, the emphasis on the man's part in reproduction was enhanced by the boys' staying in an initiation camp for 9 months, which corresponded to the woman's period of pregnancy. Both men and boys were taught that this was necessary for the birth of a child. Another way in which the man's crucial role in continuing the clan was stressed was by the men's bodies taking on a mystery equivalent to the mystery of women's reproductive processes. Thus the men had a 'secret', which was that they did not ever defecate after their initiation, and belief in this 'secret' was upheld among the women. This has been part of the reason for the slow adoption of pit latrines on the mountain — tradition upheld by the myth: no female was to see a man in the act of defecating (M.-L. Swantz, 1965, 143–4).

Such ways of stressing man's reproductive role were particularly necessary in a society which placed a high premium on the continuity of the clan through a number of male children. Although this continuity is still vital, there are other aspects of life which are competing with the reproductive functions, particularly in men's lives. Men, however, continue to use the traditional framework to enforce male authority and to secure the public roles for themselves, as far as is possible in changing conditions.

In the traditional system, at the time of the colonial invasion, public roles in the Chagga society were reserved for men. Men sat in the councils of chiefs, and even if a judicial case involved a woman, she had a male spokesman; she herself could listen to the proceedings from behind a bush or at a distance. At the same time, women exercised considerable power as mothers and sisters in the chiefly families, and records even of women chiefs are part of the Chagga history. One account related by an elder to one of the research assistants told of a daughter, Mayanka (meaning second daughter), of a *mangi* (chief) called Lokila[1], who was *mangi* of Kibosho before the coming of the Germans. Mayanka was chosen as chief because she was found to be the cleverest of Lokila's children. She ruled only for a short while and was said to have played her part well. However, the prestige of the people could not in the long run stand the reputation of being ruled by a woman. As a consequence Lokila's relative, Sina, who had been taken by the chief of Machame, was returned and made the *mangi*.

Some detail was recounted by the informant which showed that such a public role was conceived as a male role, even when it was executed by a woman. It was said that Mayanka simulated male behaviour to the extent of using a tube while urinating. One assumes that this was to emphasise that she conceived her role as a male role and herself as a female substitute for a man.

The social system of the Chagga differs from the Haya system in that it has given the wife who has married into another clan a greater role and place in that clan. Through exchange of gifts and payments of bridewealth, the husband's family has gradually acquired the right to treat the wife as a member of the husband's clan. Whether the wife is part of the husband's clan or not in the Chagga system is a matter of definition, but the wife's status in the husband's lineage is anyway fully recognised. It cannot be said, as is said in the Haya society, that the wife does not belong anywhere. She is given a social obligation towards her children's solidarity with that lineage. When the word 'clan' is used to refer to the lineage, as is generally the case, it is no more than a symbolic representation of the historical roots of the husband's lineage and of its rights to the inherited land they occupy. The clan is used as the mechanism to ensure the husband's superior birthright.

Male children must be given more meat than female children because through them the clan is built and kept healthy and strong, and male children must be given more education because they keep the benefits of it within the lineage. In families where there have been sufficient means for educating both sexes, this line of thought has not become articulated, but in poorer families to educate a female child is to give benefits to the man who marries her and to his family. A woman must not do anything which is not accepted by her husband's family, lest she be accused of causing any calamity that befalls the child. If she has deviated from the ways ordered by the husband's family, she can be accused of practising witchcraft or of intentionally harming the child.

When a woman's children are small, she can return to her father's home if there is a quarrel between her and her husband. The husband then has the duty of coming to her father and taking up the case in order to settle it. When a woman's sons come of age, her father is no longer responsible for her. The son takes over, thereby also securing the woman's loyalty to the lineage of her son and her husband. Should the husband die before the children are of age, the wife is supposed to be given her husband's plots and homestead, which she takes care of in trust for her sons. Even then she has a special interest in seeing that the husband's rights within his family are honoured.

Only as the woman gets older, in her role as mother of a married son with a family, can she begin to feel a sense of power, which she exercises on behalf of her son. Then she is less apt to think that she is benefiting another lineage and clan and can think in more personal terms of supporting her son. The son in turn has the duty of supporting his mother throughout her lifetime. In this way, as the women grow older, the system captures their support for their husband's lineage and makes use of their authority, especially in the form of the threat of the mother-in-law's curse (see below). The woman's personal benefits and the respectability of her role are now dependent on her adherence to the lineage to which she originally came as a stranger. This change that takes place in the orientation of a woman during her lifetime *serves to break up the solidarity of women as a group*. When the son marries, it is the duty of the mother to see that the young woman does not become a divisive element in the family. In any one household in which two generations live in the same compound, or even as neighbours, *the women from different generations tend to have different loyalties*. In order to minimise conflict, the traditional system provided extensive instruction to the young bride by the women from the husband's family, particularly his sister, who explained the family customs to the new wife.

One of the most concrete ways of subduing women in Chagga society has been the institution of female circumcision, which is to a degree still perpetuated. An overt reason given is the intention of preventing the wife from experiencing sexual desire for other men.

Whether clitoridectomy deprives women of sexual enjoyment, and what its physiological consequences are, will not be discussed here. However, the fact remains that circumcision has been used as a tool for subjecting a woman to the rule of her husband and for threatening a young wife should she not follow the instructions given to her. In this way many girls who in their own homes have avoided the circumcision rituals have had to submit to them in the husband's home, where the mother-in-law might not accept the young bride and her possible offspring without performing the operation on her first.

The question is posed (without attempting to answer it here) as to whether clitoridectomy as practised among the Chagga has not in fact had the intended consequence, and whether this is one of the reasons why Chagga women have not escaped their strongly-regulated and subdued lives into towns and prostitution, as the Haya women, on whom no operations are performed, have done.

At the time of the 1967 census, a much smaller proportion of Chagga women than Haya women resided in urban centres. Among the Chagga it is a common custom to leave the wife on the mountain to care for the farm while her husband works elsewhere. It is likely that the institution of circumcision has reinforced the pattern of integration of the woman into the husband's family under his and his people's dominance.

In *The Young Child Study* conducted in Moshi District (Freyhold *et al.*, 1973)., the writers expressed the view as a result of their research that there was a generation conflict between the younger and older women and that the latter used circumcision as their weapon to maintain their dominance in society or at least to hold on to a position of influence. With diminished farm sizes, the failure of coffee crops and a general decline in the living standards of the poor or only moderately prosperous peasants, the peasant woman's position is threatened more than ever before. The older women witness the decrease of the younger generation's respect for them, since the young see that their parents' ideas and ways of life are old-fashioned and also find that the older generation does not have any economic means from which the younger generation can benefit. The only way in which the old women can attempt to regain the respect of the younger is to turn to tradition and to make it operative in the present-day context. Pointing out the neglect of a particular tradition, and the grave consequences of this, is one of the ways in which the older women use their power.

During our research among the Chagga, many people — both men and women — expressed the view that a woman should not aspire to tasks which would elevate her above the male authority in the home. Both knowledge of the economic state of the husband and care of the coffee sales were generally considered to be tasks which should be left to the man. In the same way it was considered unsuitable for a woman to become a spokesman in public meetings, since public roles belonged to men, who knew how to handle such matters. However, there was recognition of the fact that some women do appear publicly in this way.

It was also considered a threat to the authority of the husband if the wife had considerable income of her own. The secretary of the Marriage Conciliation Board in Kibosho mentioned among the cases that had been handled by the Board one in which the husband had brought accusations against his wife, who earned money from beer-brewing while he did not have any regular income. 'This causes the wife to think of herself as being equal to her husband and to show it by coming home as late as the husband does.' As the wife was found to 'feel herself equal to her husband', she was given a warning by the Board and made to pay a fine to keep her in her place. This woman had taken the initiative in carrying the financial burden of looking after the family, but was not praised for it but punished instead. One cannot, of course, generalise from such a case, but the Board secretary reported it as a good illustration of what happens. It is worth noting, because this attitude towards women deters them from taking any initiative at all in the care of their households, beyond those means which are allotted to them by custom.

One of the means which is considered legitimate for women is growing and selling bananas. Everything related to bananas, whether it is peeling, cooking or carrying them, must be done by women. It is not only shameful for a man to do these jobs, but they are mostly conceived as taboo for him. Another legitimate way for a woman to get money is through selling the beans she grows, usually on the *shamba* below the mountain. Often there are not enough for selling; the beans are consumed by the family. But beans are considered to be the woman's crop. In some cases, if the woman does not obtain cash from the husband, she is tempted to sell the bean crop, even when it means that the family will be left without protein food later. The wife may think that it is the husband's duty to provide the protein food in the form of meat, and therefore she uses her only legitimate chance to get her own cash. *Kiburu*, beans cooked with banana, is considered a low-status food, especially by men.

The brewing of beer is also usually a woman's job. Conflict occurs only when the woman establishes herself in her own business, or sets herself up in a beer club as a regular brewer of beer there. This both makes demands on her time and gives her financial opportunities which threaten male authority. Whereas it is considered reasonable for a man to spend his time in beer clubs, there is general disapproval of a woman having such freedom.

Everything connected with meat, from butchering to buying it, is the task of the men. However, it has become a common occurrence to see women in the meat shops, as many men are employed away from home. The maize crop, after it has been cultivated and weeded by the women, is harvested and sold through arrangements made by the men, as is the coffee.

In all these ways the society continues to perpetuate the distinct roles of men and women. They are not only conceived as distinct but have differences in value. There seems to be little questioning among the men about the superiority of the male roles. In the patrilineal Chagga society this superiority is seen as necessary for the continuance and the health of the lineage.

To balance the one-sidedness in the family structure, the traditional system designated the second pair of children, the second male and the second female child, as the children of the mother's side. They were traditionally sent to live with the mother's parents.

When such a boy grew up, the maternal grandfather had the duty of helping him with bridewealth payments, as he also received some payments for the granddaughter at her marriage.

From the material collected for the present studies it would seem that the custom of children being sent to the grandparents may be waning, which could have the further effect of minimising the links between the father's and mother's lineages through a common concern over the children. This in turn relieves the mother's family of any responsibility for her children, even when help might be needed. A woman's mother is, however, responsible for her daughter's children born out of wedlock. According to custom, a woman could not take along to another man a child born outside a marriage.

The frequency of cases encountered in this research in which a wife had returned to her parental home when in conflict with her husband indicates that a younger woman still seeks security with her own family, but if her father has died, a woman faces difficulty. Her mother is likely to be living in what has become her son's homestead, and the daughter often has no place there. Having full status neither in her father's nor brother's homestead, the position of a woman who always has to be under some man's patronage is precarious indeed.

The children belong to the father and the father's family, unless they are the children of 'the mother's side', as explained earlier. If the mother leaves the husband's home, she is not supposed to take the children along. According to custom, however, if the mother leaves behind a nursing child the husband is supposed to send it to her to be taken care of.

In a situation in which changing conditions bring about many exceptions to the customary practice, it is easy for an individual or family to manipulate the situation to his or their own advantage. Such exceptions have always been present. No rule was ever applicable in all situations.

In present-day society, children are not always the asset they used to be; instead, they can become a burden. In such a situation the husband may refuse to recognise his responsibility towards his children. The customary Chagga law does not recognise the woman as an independent member of society with her own rights to land and property. Thus a woman who is left alone with her children does not have any recourse, should the relatives concerned be indisposed to take up their responsibility. For example, if a husband neglects his family, the extended family may feel no sense of responsibility about caring for his children. Traditionally, the woman whose husband died was 'inherited' by a brother of the husband, and her children had their father's right to the inheritance. Nowadays, however, the brother may refuse to take on such an extra burden. Thus the husband's family, oscillating between old custom and new practice, may choose to act either in favour of the daughter-in-law or against her, and will not be ostracised by the society at large if it chooses the latter course.

This means that the weak structural position of women in the traditional society leaves them without support in the changing situation. Particularly if there has been either no official marriage or no official divorce, the wife cannot claim land for herself in the name of her husband's children. In such a case, the husband's decision to disregard traditional practice leaves the wife with the children and nowhere to turn. Cases like this fall outside the structural framework of the local society. They require outside interference in the form of welfare activities, until the system of land use changes in practice and offers more equitable chances to all categories of people. In principle, the woman is recognised in the new village legislation as a person with her own rights, but in areas of land shortage the customary land rights continue to be operational.

Social control through ancestral obligation, curse and allegation of sorcery

Charles Dundas in his book *Kilimanjaro and its People* (1924, new edn. 1968) describes the curse uttered on a death-bed as the poor man's only weapon against the wealthy neighbour with whom he has come into conflict. Evidence that curse has been much used in Chagga society appears in the available literature on Chagga customs and history, as well as in the data gathered during this study. It reflects also the old roots of stratification.

Already in Dundas' time, women were known to use the weapon of curse more than men. The present data allots the curse entirely to women and usually it is pronounced over other women. Just as Dundas described it as the poor man's weapon, so it can be interpreted as an expression of the inferior social position that women hold in the society. It is the only weapon available to a woman to express her oppression and, with a means left to the powerless, to wield power. As long as curse is believed to have an effect, her weapon has some force. That the pronouncement is over other women may be a reflection of the holding to traditional beliefs being more tenacious among women than among men, but through the women the children are affected and in this way men become affected also. However, during the study at least one case was related concerning a wealthy man who was said to be fatally ill because of the curse by his mother, whom he had not cared for during her lifetime.

Another form of curse which also came up during the study is usually referred to as 'striking the pot', *kupiga chungu*. A small pot, filled with household scraps and bones over which the curse is pronounced, is hit and then buried in the ground, under a tree.[2] This can be a helpless wife's only form of rebellion when, for example, her husband had used the bridewealth money from the daughter whom she, the first wife, has brought up to adulthood, for acquiring another younger wife for himself. This is considered to be a form of suicide, and, in the case cited, striking the pot resulted, within weeks, in the death of the woman who did it.

Surviving traditional customs are a sign not only of women's conservatism, but also, as many men and women alike would express it, of their *ujinga*, ignorance or stupidity. Such customs must also be seen as the only remaining way for them to exert any power in the social situation in which they find themselves. Thus the traditional beliefs must not be taken only as something to be eradicated by education or repression; their causes must be examined and their language interpreted in terms which make removal of the causes possible.

The interests of the lineage are still supported by a system based on the authority of the parents' generation over their children's. This is clearly expressed in the system of sanctions which is upheld through the perpetuated belief in the effects of curse. In the changing social pattern, with the nuclearisation and individualisation of families and the breakdown of cooperation, the causes of illness or misfortune are sought in the use of harmful medicines with which land is treated when an individual has suffered injustice in a land dispute. From this, the next step is to accuse a neighbour or relative with whom there has been some quarrel of the use of sorcery, *mafusa*. Several older people maintained that *mafusa* was a fairly recent innovation and that they did not know much about it. An important difference between *mafusa* and a medicine treatment of the land on which a family was living was that in the case of land contamination the first to be affected would be the closest relatives — brothers, sons and others in the line of direct descent. *Mafusa*, on the other hand, was more individualistic and liable to affect any member of the nuclear family. This interpretation seems to follow the pattern of structural change in the Chagga society as well as the change in the pattern of conflict. Thus the shift from curse to the use of medicine and thence to the use of sorcery as an explanation for illness is a shift from a system of social sanctions controlling authority within a lineage towards a more individualistic control of factors which are believed to affect the life of the nuclear family.

It is interesting to note that the control by curse is allotted to women. It is the husband's mother's mother's and father's mother's curses which are feared. The causes given for such curses were related to conflicts between women of consecutive generations. They expressed themselves in food disputes, such as when a daughter-in-law neglected to feed her husband's mother after her husband had inherited his father's land; or in refusal to be circumcised or to follow the rules of the husband's clan in the care of the children. Thus duties are performed under the threat of a potential curse, and calamities are still explained by the same conflicts even after the death of the older generation.

During this research, we came across two cases where a child's illness was believed to have been caused by the father's mother, who had been heard saying during her lifetime that she would make her daughter-in-law continue to suffer. Such expressions as 'You will still see . . .' or 'You will still cry . . .' are threats which are remembered in times of difficulty, and mothers and grandmothers can also pronounce definite curses on their death-beds. Such threats by women are an expression of their own limited power when they have yielded their active power to their sons' wives. On the other hand, the fact that the threat in the society is conceived as coming from the female side, and that children's illnesses are perceived as clear evidence of the past female family members' displeasure, can be interpreted as showing the concealed power that it is feared women are able to exercise. It allows women indirect control over family affairs.

Kupiga chungu, striking a pot, was said to have been resorted to only in some very severe cases when a dispute affecting the lineage was in question. A case was related in which a current illness was supposed to derive from a past event of 'striking a pot' on the piece of land where the present family was experiencing difficulty. This, however, was refuted by two knowledgeable elders, on the grounds that the effect of striking a pot was more direct and resulted in the death of the closest family members in the direct line of descent.

Quarrels which occur between women neighbours, however, are not liable to develop into cases of curse. There are no family loyalties to uphold and no question of authority to solve. Thus problems with neighbours have to be interpreted in other terms. Here the fear develops from a situation of familiarity and potential or actual rivalry between neighbours, which may give rise to suspicion, envy and finally sorcery accusations.

Mafusa appears to have become a more general word for practices following which the victim is referred to as having been bewitched. Belief that a child may have been bewitched was expressed by many women. *Mafusa* was explained as consisting of the sorcerer's getting hold of the child's excrement, urine, hair or piece of cloth, treating it with some medicine and then placing it in a tree, digging it into the ground or throwing it into a flowing river to be carried away. Another method is for the sorcerer to swallow the matter. Whatever the case, the intention is that another *mganga*, medicine man, to whom the people concerned may go, should be unable to discover its location and thus disempower it. Such sorcery is believed to result in the swelling of the child. If the *mganga* who is asked to discover the hidden cause of the swelling finds it before the child breaks out in blisters, he is believed to have a chance of curing the child. If the blisters break out, it is too late. Thus obvious malnutrition cases were at times interpreted in these terms and not brought to a clinic.

Sorcery can be practised also by projecting an article or substance into the victim's body, and the *mganga* then has to remove it. The deceit employed in removing the substances from a patient's body was revealed by one *mganga*'s son, who described the pretence of removing offending substances from the body, while in fact taking them from where they were secreted about the *mganga*'s own person.

According to our research assistants' reports, although sorcery was practised by women, the counter-measures were in the hands of men. In a different survey, made by a student in Uru, six out of twenty-five women from different levels of income and education gave traditional medicine as their special skill (*dawa za kiyeneji*). This is assumed to be a skill which deals with herbal treatment and is handed down within families. To what extent sorcery or its counter-measures are involved in this practice is uncertain.

Relations of production

A shift in the Chagga economy to a more intensified mode of production, with the goal of maximising the profits, has been gradually brought about since the former subsistence economy has been linked up with international trade through coffee. Accelerated production has been possible through maximum utilisation of women's labour. The pre-capitalistic relations of production, based on reproduction and women's work, have been perpetuated and exploited, applying traditional norms even since the production has shifted to an individual profit-making basis.

The colonial government encouraged coffee-growing by distributing seedlings to the chiefs, and the chiefs and their families, advisors and elders were the first to develop coffee-growing and to appropriate land for cash benefits. Another category of people who developed cash-crop cultivation and enlarged their acreage were teachers. Using female labour, local teachers were able to carry out a full farming programme and use their salary, however small, for investment. The teachers were followed by traders and craftsmen, creating a diversified peasant economy. These developments were accompanied by educational opportunities offered mainly by the Lutheran and Catholic missions and later by the Native Authority. From families which could create sufficient surplus of money for school fees, young people were sent to higher schools and were soon able to supplement the already-growing income of their fathers.

Between the two World Wars, coffee was adopted as every man's crop, but because of the uneven distribution of the initial potential for creating surplus, considerable differentiation has resulted. Only a man with some initial wealth and surplus has been able to keep on acquiring new land for his second or third son and thus prevent the division of his own land into small, insufficient $\frac{1}{2}$–2 acre plots. A man with little surplus has had to divide the land at least between his eldest and youngest sons until the remaining plots are no longer capable of supporting a family. Varying figures are given as to the average size of present landholdings. According to Sender (1970), half the population has less than an acre of *kihamba* land; Brewin (1965) gives 3.2 acres as the average. With fluctuating coffee prices, and crop failures because of coffee berry disease, dependence on coffee as the sole source of cash has brought about great difficulties for the poorer peasants. The outcome has been labour migration, depleting the mountain especially of younger male population. But it has also resulted in a change in production relations. Former mutual sharing in labour has turned to wage employment, mostly on a casual labour basis. The time spent by smallholders on their agricultural activities is further reduced by the necessity to work on their wealthier neighbours' plantations.

Most wealthier farmers employ hired labourers. In 1974 in Kibosho daily payment was 5–6 shillings for about five hours of work. Coffee picking was paid according to the amount picked. Women often looked for extra income at the time of coffee picking, either on private farms or on the nationalised estates. Other work for which casual labourers were hired was pruning and spraying trees. Both male and female workers were employed during the cultivation season on the fields below the mountain, where the work was mostly done on a contract basis. Women were hired for weeding. The wealthy farmers keeping grade cattle[4] also employed people to cut out grass on the plains; the grass was then transported by pick-up trucks up the mountain. Men and women were further hired in beer clubs to brew and sell the beer, although in Kibosho most of the brewing was done in women's homes, whence it was sold to the club owners at a price dictated by the buyer. Men and women were also hired as domestic servants in the richer households.

Much of the male income is consumed by beer-drinking. It is generally assumed that a woman should be able to provide her family with food (except meat, which is the husband's responsibility), and make enough cash from small sales of banana, fruit, vegetables, beans, milk or eggs to manage the small expenses such as salt, oil and maize flour and her own and the children's necessities. This means that impoverished peasant women are constantly looking for small opportunities to earn money. Besides the forms of employment mentioned earlier, women could cut firewood in the forest and carry it down the mountain for 1.5 shillings a load. The same amount was paid in Kibosho to a woman carrying boards or loads of building poles which men cut or sawed in the forest. In order to be able to provide her family with the daily necessities, a woman may have to reduce the value of her work even further. This means that it may take half a day for a woman to earn sufficient to buy a pint of milk.

Some aspects of interdependence between the different sectors of the society still prevail. One such example is keeping cattle for a neighbour or a kinsman. Since manure is in demand and even the little milk that a zebu cow gives is highly valued, these benefits compensate for the work which caring for another man's cow gives. The arrangement also allows the client to have the second calf and thus initiate his or her own herd. The same system applies to goats and sheep. However, this kind of interdependence readily develops into dependence, and the rich farmer can use the services of his client in other ways also. A poor peasant may offer his only goat in seeking his influential neighbour's assistance in getting his child to school, or a peasant may risk losing his whole *kihamba* in pawning it to gain school fees for his children. There are many ways in which at present the pretence of mutual sharing has been turned to covert and overt exploitation. In this the poor male peasants' position equals that of women, whose labour is utilised while men determine almost completely the use of the returns of that labour.

It is my contention here that women's labour has continually been utilised as if the production were based on the principle of mutual sharing, and it still continues to be the dominating principle. The woman gives her labour as part of her family obligation, without having a share in the planning of the use of it, or in the monetary benefit ensuing from it. Women themselves have not come to a full realisation of the implications of their position, and submit to it because of the ideals inculcated in them by social norms belonging to a mode of production which no longer operates.

There is still much waste of women's labour in the daily walks up and down the mountain to cultivate on the lower *shambas*. The women still go out daily with small sickles to cut grass for the cattle. The interest in better transportation facilities and more efficient ways of cutting grass has not arisen from any concern about the strain involved for women. Improvement has come because of the introduction of grade cows for commercial production, and the better feed they require, which must be both purchased and cut in greater quantities.

The exploitation of women has also accelerated since the men have migrated for employment outside the home areas. This development has removed from the home even that part of the men's labour which was there and has transferred the total operational responsibility to the women. In such cases the woman has become a worker on her husband's farm, from which the husband extracts the profits. It was noticeable in our samples both from the ujamaa village (see below) and the old villages that the regular wage-earning husbands, particularly the professional men, kept their wives on the fields, letting them harvest the coffee, yet considering it the husband's right to reap the benefits and to manage it all. '*Kila kitu ni juu ya mume*' is a phrase used by women in such a position ('Everything depends on the husband').

The wife shoulders the responsibility for the family. How she manages this depends not only on the income level of the husband but also on his willingness to support his family. It is common that the man thinks that because his wife has her *shamba* she does not need the cash income he earns. Since the women are supposed to manage the family subsistence, men have not become fully aware of the increased strains created by higher prices and the greater number of food and utility items that have to be purchased.

In wealthy households the woman's workload is lightened by hiring domestic servants in the house and paid labourers in the fields and for cutting grass. In this case the use of hired labour frees the farm management from dependence on the woman's physiological states and makes the impersonal relationships an asset to the profit-making intentions of the farmer or business owner. Even then, those aspects of work which do not increase the cash income are left for women to do as they have been before, regardless of whether they are over-strenuous for the women or not.

NOTES

1. Stahl (1964, 162) tells of the cleverest *wife* of Lokila being chosen as the chief.
2. The information about the way the pot is hit was received by the writer in Usangi, Pare, and may be different from the Chagga custom; however, the Chagga custom as described by Dundas appears to be the same.
3. In January 1975 the Regional TANU committee decided to abolish the system of dividing land for *kihambas* (*Daily News*, 3 Jan. 1975).
4. Grade cattle = the imported, improved breed, which produces much more milk than the local breed (zebu).

4

NUTRITION AND THE SITUATION OF WOMEN IN MOSHI DISTRICT

In 1974 the people of Moshi District in Kilimanjaro were suffering from the effects of several years of drought and poor coffee yields. Government statistics showing the numbers of people requesting food assistance,[1] and statistics from the Kilimanjaro Christian Medical Center (KCMC) on the numbers of children being admitted to their clinic with severe malnutrition, seemed to indicate that the population's lower-income group had been thrown into critical levels of poverty. My own research interests were in line with the administrative and medical personnel's need to know more about the situation. How had it come about? Was the apparent malnutrition really due to the mothers' ignorance of ways of feeding, as was assumed in the District's development plan? The researchers were anxious to study the wider context of prevalent general socio-economic and environmental conditions.

A research team was organised by the Bureau of Resource Assessment and Land Use Planning (BRALUP) of the University of Dar es Salaam and the Community Health Department of KCMC. For the main part of the research, a participatory approach was employed. Cases of malnourished children who had stayed with their mothers in KCMC's Nutrition Rehabilitation Unit (hereafter NURU) were followed through close observation and participation in the daily lives of their mothers and fathers, and of their neighbours and relatives. The study, conducted over a period of three months, led in turn to a study of other related aspects, mainly the situation of women in Chagga society and the implementation of socialism in Moshi District.

'While children in Chagga are considered to be the property of their fathers, it is the mother, who under conditions of economic stress, feels responsible for their welfare and survival.' This conclusion, drawn in earlier research in Moshi District (Freyhold *et al.*, 1973, 273), needed to be further substantiated in the hope that this would in turn yield information on the amount of the women's work involved in the care and support of her family and about the problems of child care *vis-à-vis* the family's workload and the resources available to the family.

Leading members of the society, whose better lot in life may not have given them sufficient insight into the situation of their poorer neighbours, had suggested that alcoholism, ignorance and lack of

96

education were factors in what they considered women's misuse of available resources in providing for their families. To what extent was this true? In examining how much power a woman had to change her situation, the research looked at the existing efforts at self-help and cooperation as means of alleviating problems, and the extent to which a woman's economic and social status acted as a barrier to cooperation and self-help. The difference that living in an ujamaa village could make to women's lives was studied separately.

The main findings from the research are presented below in two separate sections, one concentrating on the malnutrition study and the other on women in an ujamaa village in which peasants from the mountainside came to farm. This particular village was held up by the administrative officers as the solution to the problems of landless and other poor peasants. The study was made before the enactment of the village legislation.[2]

The malnutrition study

The reason for presenting some of the findings of the malnutrition study in a book on the situation of women in Tanzania in general is to show how the various factors which have been described as characterising Chagga society — the land inheritance system, the control of cash by men, the constraints placed on women by traditional teachings and so on — can, in their extreme forms be manifested in a state of poverty, resulting in a family's inability to look after its children. The malnutrition study is intended here to be viewed in this perspective. It is important to see that if women's living conditions are not attended to, the whole society is affected by it.

Two subdivisions, Kibosho and Uru, were selected for the study, mainly on the basis of the frequency of cases referred to NURU from these areas. Other studies had shown that Kibosho represented a relatively low-income area and Uru a middle-income area (Zalla, 1974). Both were predominantly Catholic.

Forty family cases from NURU admittance records, plus two additional cases found during the study and referred to NURU, were investigated. The number of children involved was fifty-two: thirty girls, seventeen boys and five whose sex was not recorded. Selection depended mainly on the proximity of the cases to the home bases of the students who did the actual field study, except in one case: Mary Zalla, an American sociologist, did her part after a three-year residence on a nearby farm. It was decided that for each NURU case visited acquaintance would be sought with at least two other families within their immediate neighbourhood for comparative purposes. Altogether, sixty-nine neighbouring families were included, some of whom were the neighbours of more than one NURU family. Research among these families had the additional aim of obtaining neighbours' and relatives' viewpoints on the causes of the NURU children's illness and level of rehabilitation.

The study was conducted when five university students had their long vacation in April through June 1974. One student also did a follow-up study later in the year. All but one worked in their home areas. No questionnaires were used while talking with the people, and much time was spent participating in the daily life of the affected families and in contacting the local political and administrative leaders as well as some Church workers.[3]

Factors affecting nutrition

Some of the factors responsible for malnutrition were evident from the records of the rehabilitation centre and from observations made by its personnel in conducting follow-up home visits. Often named by health workers as causes were both fathers' and mothers' alcoholism, broken homes, the mother's inability and ignorance in caring for her children, frequent births, land shortage, traditional beliefs, and a lack of cooperation between people in the community. These were investigated in detail.

It soon became evident that no single factor could be isolated as being solely responsible for the deteriorating level of nutrition. Such causes as the mother's drunkenness and, in some cases, the mother's mental retardation, or the father's illness and consequent inability to support his family, do not in themselves offer sufficient explanation. Numerous questions arise. What causes the mother to drink or to be incapable of caring for her family? Why cannot the society support a sick father, and what, in any case, is the root-cause of his illness? What is the capacity of the society to take care of emergencies, and is this capacity evenly distributed? Further, why are traditional beliefs held by some and not by others? What are these beliefs, and in what way may they become detrimental to the weaker members of the society? What means did the traditional society employ to provide care for its weaker members, and how have changes in the society affected these means of social security?

The economic situation of the society was assumed to be the underlying cause of malnutrition. To what extent was the apparent stratification in the society evidence of a developed class system? The family economy had to be analysed in relation to the changing patterns of inheritance and land ownership as well as the dominance of the cash economy over traditional forms of cooperation. This in turn was linked to the study of larger questions of economic dependence upon the international market systems and the policies of the country.

The family economy

Land ownership. It has already become evident that the land inheritance system is a decisive factor in the lives of individuals in Chagga society. Inherited land is often divided into such small plots that families find it difficult to live solely on what they can grow there. Of the 42 NURU families, almost a quarter had less than an acre of coffee-banana land. The average amount of land per family was 1.4 acres, whereas enquiries among neighbours showed that the average farm size otherwise in the locality was 2.3 acres.

There was evidence of reluctance on the part of some fathers to hand over land to their sons. The family system had become nuclear to the degree that parents began to doubt that their children would support them if they should face some hardship when ageing. The custom had been for fathers to hand over, while still alive, at least their eldest sons' part of the inheritance. But with increasing commodity prices, the threat of poor crops due to coffeeberry disease, and the low market price of coffee, elderly people were afraid to part with their own security.

On the other hand, there were cases in which the youngest son was hesitant to leave the inherited homestead, even when he was living in conditions of hardship. The duty of the youngest son to remain in the homestead was emphasised over and over again. The previously described parental curse and the fear of misfortune that might befall a son neglecting his duty still acted as a powerful sanction. A man working away from home might even keep his wife on the mountain because he could not break with the obligation placed on him by custom to keep the lineage inheritance in his possession and to care for it. The parents of one of the NURU children had been living and working in Tabora but had returned on the death of the man's father to take care of the home *kihamba* and to fulfil his duty as the youngest son. The wife was unhappy, but said they could not do otherwise in the given situation, although the bequeathed land was only half an acre.

Family Income. Most of the NURU families had no regular additional sources of income to supplement their small coffee income. They received only a little extra support from members of their families who worked outside the home area and none from relatives who were living at home but working away.

While thirty-seven of the NURU fathers were said to be farmers, twenty-two of them relied on casual labour for their main income. At the time of the study the opportunities for such work were very poor. Eight fathers got some income from self-employment activity.

NURU mothers were generally described as cultivators working on the family *shamba*. Some, however, were trying to get extra income of their own by selling bananas or other produce, brewing beer, working in their father-in-law's compound or as casual labourers on the nearby coffee estates. Twenty-one NURU women said that they were totally dependent on the money their husbands gave them, which in most cases had been earned through hired labour. Eleven families were living on the incomes of both parents. Three mothers were dependent on relatives and five were supporting themselves and their families.

Some information on the women's ability to manage money matters was obtained from seventeen NURU mothers. Only two were reported as knowing the family and farm income and as managing money matters together with their husbands. Five were able to manage money matters and had some knowledge of their husband's income, while five others earned their own money and managed their income. Information on this point about the NURU mothers is incomplete. The common dependence on the husband's income indicates that the wife is intentionally kept ignorant of financial matters. However, women do handle household money and sell their own produce, but they keep quiet about it for fear that this might also be taken away from them.

Fourteen of the NURU mothers said that they received money from their husbands for buying daily food. In only four cases did the husband buy the household necessities, a custom which is prevalent on the coast. Apart from the five that earned their own money, the rest of the women suffered from the irregularity or lack of support by their husbands.

Social factors affecting parents' ability to care for their children

Sixteen of the NURU wives complained that the cause of their children's problems was the father's irresponsibility or sheer neglect in providing money or caring for the family. In five of the cases, the problems were attributed to the father's alcoholism and in five other cases to his illness. Altogether, the father's drinking was found to be a major problem in twelve of the NURU families. People's own estimates of whom they considered heavy drinkers, which were recorded, indicated that a greater proportion of NURU fathers than neighbouring fathers were heavy drinkers. The effects of heavy drinking were particularly serious for the low-income families, since a wealthier man can afford to drink and support his family whereas the father of a poorer family can afford only one or the other. The poor condition of the family affects people's opinions of the parents, while in a wealthier family the heavy drinking may go unnoticed and more easily be recorded as moderate.

Some District Party and Church leaders saw the increase in excessive drinking by mothers as a major problem in the District; it was found to exist in six of the NURU families and in only one neighbouring family. In general, however, husbands were said to drink moderately while wives were said to drink little, and this was verified through observation. However, even moderate drinking in poorer families became detrimental to children's health when compounded with other factors. Women's drunkenness brings moral disapproval, while men's drinking is taken as a matter of course. This explains why drunkenness in women is so conspicuous.

The mothers' capacity to care for their families was in two cases limited by their state of mental deficiency. Five of the mothers were pregnant at the time of the study, which prevented them from doing heavy work in the fields. One mother had partly abandoned her children, for reasons that did not become clear; she was blamed by neighbours for sheer neglect.

Family pattern

Marriage and the nuclear family unit. The families in which malnutrition had occurred displayed a marked degree of marital stability, in spite of the prevailing problems. In all cases but one, the alliance between the father and mother of the children had been a union of some permanence. In 37 families, all the children in the family were of one father. In the other families there had been two fathers. Only four of all the families studied reported having children of relatives. The small number of families caring for the children of an extended family, formerly a common occurrence, demonstrates the growing importance of the nuclear family in Chagga society. The sense of family responsibility is increasingly limited to the nuclear family, and only extended to lineage responsibilities on conditions of mutuality, as will be shown later.

Another indication of decreased familial responsibility is the weakening tie between generations. Under strained economic conditions, both the grandparents' generation and that of their children were found to give priority to personal advantage over family responsibilities, and where the family responsibility of caring for children's children conflicted with personal advantage, the latter took precedence. The case of withholding land and possessions has already been mentioned. Similarly, a child in the grandparents' house could be considered a liability rather than an asset. The mother of either the child's father or mother might refuse such responsibility unless it either relieved her of some of the domestic work or brought in cash paid by the child's mother to compensate for the feeding of the child. Low-income families could not provide the grandparents with this kind of extra cash, which may be one of the reasons why there were only five cases of children living with their paternal or maternal grandparents, even though it has been a common Chagga custom that the eldest boy and girl should go to live with the paternal grandparents and the second pair with the maternal grandparents. Similarily, only two children were living with relatives away from home.

One malnourished child had been left in the care of the maternal grandmother when the child's mother got married to a man other than the child's father. The grandmother was looking after two children of an unmarried daughter at the same time and was unable to manage them all. In another case, the grandmother was looking after five children of two unmarried daughters, who paid for their care. Three children of a son, whose wife had returned to her parental home, were added to these. As a consequence, the youngest, who had not yet been weaned, became malnourished. In this case, the son had not contributed in cash toward the feeding of the children, nor had he permitted the nursing mother to take the child with her. In yet another case, the child's maternal grandmother would have been willing to care for the children whom her daughter could not care for properly, but the grandfather forbade her to take on the responsibility because the husband had not finished his marriage payments. The daughter was considered mentally retarded both by the neighbours and by the staff in the Rehabilitation Unit.

Frequency of births. In the families where malnutrition had occurred, mothers with an average age of 30 years had had an average of 4.9 births. Only one of the NURU mothers was over 40 and the youngest was 21. The neighbouring mothers had had an average of 5.5 births. The fact that they had a higher average of births than NURU mothers can be explained by their greater ages: twenty-five were over 40 years old. The fertility rate for rural mainland Tanzania according to the 1967 census was 6.7 and for the Kilimanjaro Region 7.9 (Egero & Henin, 1973). While it is difficult to draw firm conclusions from these figures, the fact that NURU mothers had had as many as 4.9 live births at a relatively early age and that Chagga women generally begin childbearing late and continue into middle age suggests that they may well have above-average fertility rates, even for the Region.

There is some evidence that nutrition problems were seldom present with the first child, but began with the second and subsequent children. In most cases there was another child younger than the one suffering from malnutrition. Most often, post-weaning feeding was inadequate when the mother had stopped breast-feeding the child after becoming pregnant again. In ten NURU families, children had been born in consecutive years, while in all the other NURU families with several children the births had been at two-year intervals. However, even spacing the births to every second year causes too-early weaning and leaves the older child without an adequate diet.

Traditionally, both male and female young people were taught at puberty that two-year intervals should be left between pregnancies. Fathers can still be chastised by their companions under a disguise of joking for making their wives pregnant while still nursing. The need to space children is given as a reason for the existing pattern where the man had his own house on the family compound. The wife in some cases slept with the children in the traditional house. It was also said that in some clans herbal medicines were used in order to prevent conception, information on this medicine being passed on as special knowledge pertaining to the clan.

Among mothers there was a readiness to discuss with the researchers and the staff in MCH clinics the possibility of modern family planning and some men were also agreeable to it.[4] However, a woman would usually feel subjugated among her husband's kin, a position she freely acknowledged as a divinely-ordained necessity. Since woman was created to be a 'slave' and the bearer of many hardships, she could not defy this fate although she would often say this in a defiant tone of voice. Frequency of childbirth also reduced the women's participation in work, partly because of the Chagga custom of keeping a mother inside the hut for three months after giving birth. Even when not observed fully, frequent nursing periods affected the amount of food grown for family use.

Patterns of eating

There are customary patterns of eating which, in the changed economic situation, result in an inadequate protein intake among small children. These patterns, when followed, determine both the distribution of food and the amounts and types of food eaten on the following basis:[5]
— In the distribution of food, preference was given to male adults, secondly to male children, then to female adults and children. With this kind of order of preference the small children who had just been weaned did not always get the attention they needed. These

categories of family members might eat from separate plates and even in separate places.

— Food was divided into men's and women's foods, different foods being considered suitable for each sex.

— It was taken for granted, and many still considered it an ineradicable Chagga custom, that husbands must be served a lot of meat by their wives.

The men who were asked about this last custom supported it with such reasons as that they followed what they had seen their mothers doing for their fathers. 'A man butchers the cow, a woman cannot do it. So it is also his right to eat it.' Women could eat such foods as banana and green vegetables (*kitalo*), gruel (of *mbege*, a kind of millet), sugar cane and mangoes, which men could not, so why shouldn't men have their particular food too? Children could also eat beans if they did not get meat. Because men and boys do the butchering and the purchasing of meat, their right to consume it is not questioned, at least not by the men themselves.

The Chagga woman is taught about food at the time of her circumcision, which traditionally takes place before marriage. Thus the preferential eating pattern in favour of men has traditional roots of which the women are still very much aware. The reasoning is that male children build the clan whereas a female is married to another family and will benefit another clan.

The customary teaching that affects the pattern of breast-feeding during pregnancy has already been referred to. If the husband's mother holds on to the custom, she controls the actions of the daughter-in-law, so that the young mother who might be ready to follow the teachings of the clinics and continue breast-feeding after becoming pregnant would not dare to do so, because she would be told that it would kill the child. Should something happen to the child, the mother would be accused of killing the child, who belongs to her husband's family. One mother in the sample was ostracised by her husband's family because it was believed that she had drawn the curse of the father-in-law's deceased wife on her child. It was considered harmful both to a child and to the clan to nourish the child with what was believed to be polluted milk.

When the families were asked about their food consumption, they reported the amounts of meat consumed daily, or thrice/twice weekly; the amounts stated seemed improbably large. However, because of consumption patterns, women and small children might have a very small share of the meat or none at all. In any case, men do not generally consider meat to be children's food. Furthermore, cooked or roasted meat is often tough, which makes it difficult for small children to chew.

The degree of favour a woman enjoys in the eyes of her husband, especially in a polygynous household, depends on how she pleases him with food. This in turn influences the husband's generosity in providing the necessary meat for cooking. Should the wife try to increase the amount of meat going to the rest of the family, she may defeat her purpose, for husband may then eat in a beer club instead of bringing meat home, and the children are then left with little or no meat. In a beer club a man may also obtain blood and meat soup, known popularly by such nicknames as *kisusie* or *aspro* (Freyhold *et al.*, 1973, 10). A drunken husband may demand to eat the meat he brings home with him even though he has already eaten at the club. During the study, an incident of meat poisoning which occurred in Uru illustrates the point made. Fifty people who had shared in meat-eating after slaughtering a cow were brought down to the hospitals in Moshi in a very poor condition. There was only one woman among them, the rest being men and boys.

Milk is not consumed as plentifully now by all as it was in former times. This was generally recognised by most people interviewed, who explained that the number of cows kept by individual households had decreased. Milk production was also greatly reduced during the dry season because of the shortage of fodder. Cows were milked mainly after calving and the local breed did not continue giving milk for long. On the other hand, an increased number of an improved breed of cattle affected the total production but did not necessarily add to local consumption of milk.

One of the crucial factors leading to an impoverished diet had been a decrease in cattle ownership. One older person after another related how in the past more people had kept cows and any one family had had a larger number of livestock, both goats and cows. This was possible because there had been more open spaces for grazing and good-quality grass. With the increase in coffee-growing and the change from dairy products to this cash crop, the land could no longer produce the necessary food either for people or for animals.

The older people reported that in the past one could always depend on obtaining milk without paying. If a person's own cow was not producing milk, one could get it from the neighbours on the understanding that this generosity would be reciprocated. People thought of milk production not in terms of money but rather as food. An elderly woman suggested that the non-availability of milk was the reason why older women had begun to drink *pombe*, locally brewed beer. *Pombe* served the same purpose as milk in giving bodily strength. Walking up and down the mountain ridges and valleys was so strenuous that one could not do it without some strengthening ingredient. Even small children could be given *pombe* as food. A middle-aged man, discussing questions of diet, pointed out that if a man ate the type of food that women eat (*kitalo, uji*, gruel, milk food etc.) he would be told that he was eating hunger-food, and this would lower his status. Further, he could not drink *pombe* if he filled his stomach with milk foods, and a man cannot live without *pombe*. The man maintained that the effects of the lack of *pombe* can already be seen in older men who can no longer buy as much of it as they need because of the increased prices and lack of money in the area. 'The old men have started getting thinner.' The amount of beer consumed daily by Chagga men is measured in gallons. 'A man cannot live through a week without *pombe*' was a common expression. *Pombe* was also thought to be good for nursing and pregnant women.[6] There were no complaints about side-effects, such as liver ailments brought on by excessive intake of alcohol, although its social effects on the family were mentioned. Its potential health-reducing quality was minimised because of the momentary vigour gained.

In families where malnutrition had occurred, fewer cattle were kept than the average for the area, and milk was scarce. The small amount of milk that people had was being sold by those who should have been using it in their own families because of shortage of cash and inequality of wealth. A higher level of milk consumption was noticed in wealthier households, which were not caught up in the cycle of poverty. Thus in the poorer households the needs of the day forced them to use any means available to obtain cash that day, despite the new problems this produced in the days ahead. The wealthier farmers can afford to keep grade cattle and could thus have enough milk both for home consumption and for sale.

Commercialisation of cattle-keeping has led to slaughtering and milking mainly for market purposes. One of the consequences of this has been the end of the old practice of sharing with neighbours. Where there was sharing, it now tended to follow class lines. This affected the nutritional status of poor children. The economic inequity was coupled with custom. The early weaning due to pregnancy necessitated getting cow's milk for the infant, and when this was not possible for financial reasons, problems occurred.

In earlier times, banana mixed with plenty of milk was the main diet for a young child after weaning. With milk difficult to obtain, only banana is left. Since all the Chagga from time immemorial have grown up on banana, the thought that banana might not be a suitable food for a child seems to them absurd. There is no general awareness that banana on its own is a poor-quality staple food. However, traditionally the diet was varied; a father, when told by a visiting nurse of the need for a mixed diet, said that traditionally people were taught to eat different kinds of food.

When the economic conditions are sufficiently favourable for the needs of men *and* women *and* children to be satisfied, the pattern of distribution, division and eating of foods does not become detrimental; a nutritional balance can be maintained. When economic conditions change, this balance becomes upset and the resulting problems are felt first by women. Women have carried the greater part of the burden in the past too, and as long as they have tolerated the load of work, reproduction and inequality, the society has continued. But in the new situation, not only do women live under increased pressure but the signs of that pressure are more and more impressed on their children. Yet the causes of malnutrition have not always been analysed in relation to economic inequalities and their effect on women's situation. More often than not, nutritional problems are dealt with as an educational task directed toward women.

Neglect of traditional obligations in relation to nutrition

The study showed that some people attributed the symptoms of malnutrition to neglect of traditional obligations, thus diverting attention from the real causes of the problem. To redress its anxiety and the sense of having been guilty of neglect, the family of a child in hospital might go through some sacrificial rites after the child had returned home, or they might treat the child with traditional medicines before taking him or her to the hospital or rehabilitation centre. These measures are necessary because of the interdependence of the people, not only in effecting a cure but in penetrating the root-causes of an illness, which were interpreted as deriving from conflicts in interpersonal relationships.

On one occasion symptoms of malnutrition were traced to a grandmother's curse, and required sacrifice and treatment by a *mganga*, healer, on behalf of the affected people. Another malnourished child was said to have become ill because the mother had nursed the child while being pregnant yet unaware of it. Another child's death was attributed to the failure to circumcise the mother, thus transgressing the will of the husband's mother. Similarly the failure of a man to pay the bridewealth to his wife's family was thought to be an offence against the lineage obligations which had resulted in illness — which the clinic diagnosed as due to malnutrition. In another case there was a threat that ancestor spirits would intervene if a wife had tried to benefit from the coffee earnings without her husband's knowledge. Thus tradition was used to circumscribe a woman's life with sanctions and bind her in a way which affected the welfare of her children.

The plight of peasant women

Turning from the specific question of malnutrition, one may ask more generally what opportunities are open to an impoverished peasant woman in the present situation. The evidence from Uru and Kibosho showed that cooperation and sharing could not be sought across the economic strata of a local community.

In many families sharing was still common on such occasions as a death in the family or the celebration of confirmation or marriage. At the time of a death, women from the neighbourhood would come to help in the wailing, in preparing food, carrying water and firewood, and supporting the bereaved family. However, it followed from the nature of such activities that a household which had nothing to share and little means for mourning or celebrating could hardly make it a communal affair.

Both the wealthier and the poorer people in Central Kilimanjaro quite openly said that help can be given to a poor neighbour only once or twice, but after that a relationship of dependence is born if one partner is in constant need. This had prevented the needy individuals from seeking cooperation or even employment. We found that a mother with five children of five years and under, some severely malnourished, could not get anyone to help her take the children to a clinic because they had to be carried most of the way. The only neighbour prepared to offer assistance was one who was in the same predicament. In Uru an old man was found lying with open sores, literally rotting away; an impoverished woman neighbour occasionally took him some cooked banana, but the man was no one's responsibility. (Eventually, through the Party office, some attention was paid to his case.)

Successful cooperative activities conducted by women were the kind that demanded initial capital from the participants. The Kibosho cooperative shop and village 'hotel' was in a sound financial position and had given its members an income of several hundred shillings. Cooperative bread-baking and beer-brewing had also flourished in Kibosho, but because of the capital required the poorest sector of the community could not benefit from these activities. The poorer women considered the UWT-organised cooperative shop a privilege for the better-off. Nor could a young mother tied down to her daily toil and small children gain from such cooperation. Our discussions with the poorer women revealed that the prevalent attitude was one of resignation to the constraints placed on them. Poor married women with children looked at the options they had and found no way of changing their position.

One of the things that prevented women from making efforts to improve their situation was the realisation that their husbands could make them suffer for doing so, out of their fear that the women would become economically too independent. Beating was mentioned particularly often. However, in discussions about a husband's beating of his wife, the opinion was also expressed that when beaten the wife at least knows that the husband cares enough for her to bother to punish her. When it could be demonstrated that the wife was at fault, the local Marriage Conciliation Board[7] recognised the husband's right to punish the disobedient wife, although he was warned not to mistreat her. Because the wife's position was considered that of a minor, the husband was seen as having the right to expect obedience from her and he could consider it his duty to punish her for any breach of obedience. Since these values were inculcated in the society, both by the traditional value system and through the teachings of the local churches, the woman felt helpless in the face of them, and she would often accept them herself.

A particular value system is a supportive force in society for as long as it provides an interpretation of reality acceptable to that society. It prescribes a certain moral norm which has a stabilising effect. In Chagga society the value system has developed within the framework of the patrilineal social system, which has used strong customary sanctions to uphold itself, and many of the existing values related to the emphasis on male authority have been strengthened by the local Catholic Church. The teachings in the local churches do not necessarily reflect the official position of the Church at large, but the national clergy are part of the male-oriented society and have combined their traditional background with appropriate elements from the Old Testament. Often the people's interpretation is a popular version of the teachings of the Church. In the women's minds the strong male emphasis is linked to teachings and authority of the Church as much as it is to their own social system.

The national society is currently exerting influences through the political programme of ujamaa, which aims at creating an equitable social and economic system but also at raising the position of women and giving them a fair return for the workload they carry.

The value system may gradually change through external and internal pressures in such a way that the traditional ideological props of male authority become inadequate. Socialist programmes are designed to offer women a more equitable return for their work, and this occurs in those ujamaa villages where the women are paid individually for their labour. If the husband thinks he can depend on his wife's work to cultivate his share in the communal field he is disappointed, because he finds his wife reaping the financial benefits from her agricultural input. A similar structural change is conceivable also on the mountain where, for example, the banana-selling and beer-brewing could be made cooperative enterprises controlled by women, since the prevailing system assigns both these tasks to women anyway. This would be a case where outside intervention could bring such economic pressure on the men that they would have to re-consider their cultural position.

On the other hand, the pessimistic attitude adopted by women has some justification in that the change in values cannot be brought about by people who themselves are entrenched in the existing value system. Just as it is rare for the wealthy to start working against their own interests and *voluntarily* to change their private enterprises into cooperative efforts, so it is difficult too for the men to work for change in the system of banana-selling or beer-brewing, knowing that it would affect one of their most vital social institutions, the beer club and beer-drinking. From this it follows that mere politicising is not enough to bring about change in the ideological basis of the society. An example was given earlier of a woman who was fined for her initiative in beer-brewing, since she was thought to have an arrogant spirit. The husband brought an accusation against her because she had gained self-determination through her financially-improved position. Although this was an isolated example, it indicates the direction in which the society has found itself going in relation to the position of women. It demonstrates the potential for economic leverage that women can bring to bear upon the situation.

The question is whether change can come about in a constructive manner — or through a struggle which causes at least temporary dislocation and social disintegration. The pressures created by economic practices which push sections of people to the margins, be they women or poor male peasants, may well become the effective force for necessary change. With the shortage of land the traditional means of gaining an income become more and more difficult. Women will be forced to experiment with new ways of gaining an income, even if initially they think it impossible.

The women have the potential for gaining considerable power within their allocated roles. Whether they will be driven to use that power depends on the readiness of the society to alter its cultural position. The potential for developing communal and cooperative forms of women's business has demonstrated itself in successful efforts at different locations on the mountain. It appears that women have less initial resistance than men to working together. Reluctance to work together is often due to inexperience in managing finances rather than to the idea of cooperation itself.

Women represent a great potential reservoir of human resources which has been hitherto largely ignored. The efforts to accelerate development have so far been directed toward peasants, who have been thought of as being men. Yet the peasant women have had the capacity and will to work which is not always present in a sustained form among men. The externally induced development efforts *have to consider the women's needs and not to add to their already excessive constraints*. At present production suffers because the cost of development in added women's labour hours and in the decreasing number of working women left in the villages has not so far been realistically analysed.

Women's struggle for economic independence

Circumstances limit and constrain women's lives, and as a result many women have asserted themselves and gained a measure of economic and social freedom so as to be able to manage the given situation.

Some women on the mountain have moved from cultivation into trade where they have gained an independent income. Some have also continued cultivation if they have been left in charge of their husband's land after his death, becoming small capitalists with the same kind of managerial position as the male farmers who have taken up trading or started a transport business, and have employed others to do the farm work. The increasing number of women who come down the mountain in the mornings to go to the town market to sell bananas and other fruit is clear evidence that women have started marketing their banana crop themselves. Banana sales at the local village markets have always been entirely in women's hands because of the men's refusal to join in such business, considering it a humiliation for a man to stand at the village market and sell this 'women's crop'. Men, however, have been the majority of the buyers; they have then made their profit transporting the banana stalks in bulk to town and city markets, having bought them for half of the price they obtain for it below the mountain. But there were some women who each bought four or five stalks from other women, then took them on the bus down the mountain and came back with a clear daily profit. Organising the banana sales and transport on a cooperative basis and keeping the business in the hands of the women, from the field to the distant markets, would have the effect of increasing the returns for the women concerned, which they need if they are ever to have more say over their own and their children's wellbeing.

In the same way, organising the beer-brewing activities on the mountain as a cooperative women's business would keep control in women's hands. As it was, the beer club owners controlled the price of the beer which the women brewed each day. Apart from a few clubs where the same women brewed the beer from one day to the next, the more common arrangement was for women from various houses to take turns. The owner kept the price of the beer low by *keeping the women in competition with one another.* As some of the women explained, 'If I refuse to sell my beer at that price there are others who will, and I only lose my business.' Furthermore, the club owner could refuse to buy the beer which a woman had brewed that day. His reason could well have been that he knew he would have little business on that day, but he would use the excuse that the beer was of poor quality. Sometimes the women found that the price offered was so low that they could not afford the loss, and they then tried to sell the beer privately, risking an even greater loss. In a society where women cannot openly defy male authority, they have no other way than staying quiet. However, economic necessity will eventually force them to break the conventions.

Educated women are gaining a degree of self-determination within the society. In the course of this research we communicated with numerous women in high administrative positions and in the teaching and nursing professions, who during the years had benefited from the education which the people in Moshi District on the whole have been eager to pursue. There were also women who had established themselves as independent traders, especially in the eastern parts of the District. In Moshi and Arusha towns others were running flourishing transport or tailoring businesses quite independently, supporting their families, living in houses they themselves owned and giving their children an education, even in private institutions where the fees were high. Women's economic activities and attainment of senior posts not only have the effect of enhancing their own self-esteem and self-awareness, but also convince men that women are capable of taking up roles which were previously considered exclusively in the male domain. The rural women in Kibosho and Uru recognised that there were women who had high posts in public service and in politics, not least the Member of Parliament for Uru, Lucy Lameck. In Kibosho, one ten-house cell leader was a woman. But too often these cases were still treated as exceptions, and those who achieved success had not yet changed other women's self-image and sense of their own potential.

The impact of the image of outstanding women is reduced by the fact that the educated women mostly leave the rural community, and their contacts with their own villages thereafter are only sporadic. They free themselves to a considerable degree from the values which dominate their home communities, and become attached to new wider national structures. This decreases the possibility of their influencing their own society, since they themselves are no longer considered part of that society. The students who did the research were themselves acutely aware of the differences which existed between their own values and patterns of behaviour and those of their village relatives.

The long discussions carried out with women during this research demonstrated that village women could be prompted to examine in a critical way topics related to their position, but the raised consciousness of their own situation which results can become an additional burden if it does not lead to positive action to break free of the pressures concerned. My own view is that the prevailing dissatisfaction needs to be accompanied by self-awareness so that women will begin to use the opportunities which *are* open to them. This is the case whether the dissatisfaction arises from the economic impasse in which they find themselves or whether they become aware of their own potential through a process of education and politicisation.

Women in an ujamaa village

Mtakuja, a village about 10 miles south of Moshi, serves here as a case study of an ujamaa village born already before the intensified drive for villagisation. Even if Mtakuja had not gained the status of an ujamaa village, it does have characteristics that were common to many development villages on which research has been conducted. As the land shortage on the mountain slopes becomes acute as a result of its division through inheritance into ever smaller plots, people have been forced to move out to look for other areas to cultivate. The Mtakuja village population was partly made up of such people. Plantation workers from the nearby sugar and sisal estates formed another part, securing their share of benefits in the village farm in addition to the income from wage labour. In this situation the village provided a degree of security for specific categories of people of whom women formed a significant fraction.

Mtakuja village started in 1970, when the backing of the waters of Nyumba ya Mungu Dam caused floods in the former village of Samanga, where most of the initial Mtakuja inhabitants had been living. Another village, Chekeleni, shared with Mtakuja some of the facilities including the school.

In June 1974, when the case-study was made, Mtakuja village was said to have about 157 members, but the exact numbers were difficult to check since some of the members did not live in the village, but only came there to cultivate. There were 65 women registered independently from their husbands as members — the rest came under their husbands' names — and of the 65 there were 40 who did not live with their husbands. Contacts were established with 40 of the independently registered women, who gave a good picture of women's participation in the village activities and of their lives in general. Five of them had not yet moved into the village, but were cultivating there, living nearby and waiting until Mtakuja was ready to build more houses for its members.

The government helped the people to move after the flood disaster in Samanga: besides helping with transport, materials were provided for building a sizeable storage shed, an office, a courtroom, a chicken shed and so on. The villagers had been given free food deliveries at the time of their greatest need. When our study was in progress, each working family, regardless of size, received one *debe* (about 20 litres) of maize flour per week. The village had also received help in ploughing the village-cooperative fields. Piped water had been installed in the village, but at the time of our study the waterworks were out of operation and water had to be carried from a ditch $1\frac{1}{2}$ miles away. The poor condition of the road leading to the village was said to be the reason why workmen had not come to repair the water system, yet it had been possible to bring four lorryloads of school students on a Saturday from Moshi town to work in the village fields! Such inconsistencies, among others, made an observer often sceptical of the bureaucrats' and technocrats' role in directed development.

There were 125 acres allotted to communal farming of cotton and maize, and besides this each household had its own private plot, which in the sample of 40 women's fields averaged 2.1 acres. Communal work was done four times a week for three morning hours, the rest of the time being spent in other chores and on the private plots around the houses. Women did the communal work more faithfully than men, but part of the reason for this was the men's outside employment. The daily attendance ranged from 25 to 50 women and 18 to 30 men. The highest amount paid to a woman for communal labour was quoted as 350 shillings a year (equalling one month's minimum wage), but most got much less than that. Women, in particular, felt that having a daily quota of work was a better system than having a set work schedule, because they were thus enabled to carry out their communal work quickly and go on with household chores while still leaving time for work on individual plots.

It seemed that by living in the village, many families secured a regular food supply, either from cultivation or from the periodical food assistance given, while the husband earned cash income outside the village. The sample showed that 8 of the 26 husbands had regular employment, and 16 were listed as farmers. But the proximity of the sugar plantation made it possible for many to engage in seasonal labour.

The village also received labour input from the outside from time to time, particularly from Moshi town and some locations on the mountain. One gained a strong impression that Mtakuja ujamaa village was at the time a showpiece of Kilimanjaro ujamaa efforts, where the props could be seen only too well. However, there were other encouraging aspects of village development, particularly from the women's point of view, as became evident in discussions with the 40 women. They appreciated their relative economic independence and opportunity to take part in decision-making.

The people of the Mtakuja and Chekeleni villages were from a large number of different ethnic backgrounds. The 40 women represented twelve tribal groups from neighbouring and central Tanzanian areas, the Chagga being the largest group. The migratory character of these people was evident from the family histories, which also reflected considerable marital instability compared with the more stable situation on the mountain above Moshi. Another aspect of village composition was the large number of women who were heads of households, although on the mountain the idea of a woman as head of a household was rare. In the sample, 14 (35%) of the women were heads of their own households. Nine of them were divorcees, and 4 were widows. One husband was old and had to be taken care of, as was another husband who had tuberculosis. Counting those husbands who were employed outside the village, half the households had women supporting their families. The dominance of women in household and farm management was evident.

When the village was started, most of the registered founding members were men — a common phenomenon which has been observed in other places as well. Men are the first to find out what benefits they can get out of a new experiment; the hard part, carrying the experiment through the difficult and critical period, is left for women, who have been so well trained by the hardships of life that they have the perseverance which is needed to get through the difficult stages of development. If it turns out successfully, the men turn up again to reap the benefits. Soon after the beginning, the active members in cooperative cultivation in Mtakuja were women, and after an initial experience where the men collected payments for the women's labour, the women became conscious of the importance of being registered members and collecting the returns on their own work.

Considerable consciousness of the right of each worker to receive the returns for her labour was expressed in comments such as '*Siku hizi hakuna kumpa bwana fedha, kila mtu anajitegemea*' ('These days there is no more giving of money to the husband, everyone is self-reliant') and '*Sikutaka unyonyaji nikapewa yangu mwenyewe*' ('I did not want exploitation and I was given my own plot'). Only two of the 40 women said that the husband sold the crops, and four of the women did not sell anything and cultivated only for food. One of them had some crops of her own from her 1 acre after cultivating the husband's 3 acres, but the other one expressed her dependence in the words '*Kila kitu ni mume*' ('Everything belongs to the husband'); she also worked on the communal fields on behalf of her husband, who was the registered member.

It is significant that the two women whose husbands sold the crops and who were thus dependent on their husbands for the fruit of their own labour, were the wives of regular wage-earners (a butcher and a watchman in the sugar plant). Information from the mountain showed the same trend. Although there were examples of husbands allowing their wives to get their share of the proceeds, there were at the same time an alarming number of working men who kept their wives as farm workers and controlled the income; such wage-earners who lived in the village often bought the daily necessities themselves instead of giving money to their wives. In this respect one can see the ujamaa village development offering women a fairer share from their own labour; a consequence of this is the loosening of the marriage bond because the woman is not compelled to be tied to her husband for all her needs but has the possibility of establishing an independent household of her own. A more equal relationship will require another kind of foundation for marriage than economic dependence if it is still to thrive after the wife gains financially. Breakdown in marriages needs to be interpreted by the society as a warning of the social disintegration which results from the imbalance in relations between the sexes.

Of the households interviewed, 77% had 2 acres or less of individual land. The rest were divided evenly between those who had under 4 acres and those with 5–7 acres of cultivated land. Of the 40 women, 25 joined in the communal work fairly regularly; those who were ill, pregnant or had just had babies were excused temporarily from work without any compensation. Some women had their children and mothers working in their place on the communal plot, while they themselves cultivated the family *shamba*. One woman, who was divorced from her husband, took care of the chickens of the village and was excused from the communal works in the fields. The chickens had previously been managed by one man after another, but because of the losses and disappearance of money a woman was chosen instead, with better results. In many other villages women were considered more trustworthy than men in cooperative dealings. But there were aspects beyond the control of either sex. At the time of the study, the chicken project was suffering from the poor quality of purchased chicken feed, a complaint which was also heard on the mountain slopes at that time.

No special attention was paid to pregnant women, to mothers who had recently given birth, to old people or to sick people, as had been hoped for in an ideal fully developed village. No day-care centre had yet been started. Since even the flour distribution depended on the labour input, it meant that at the time of the village striving to become self-reliant, the old and weak were left without support, except for what they received from their own families. Those mothers in particular who were the sole supporters of their families complained of this arrangement, since they lost the benefits for the time they rested during confinement.

In general, most women gave negative answers to the question about the existing cooperation between the villagers. The village was composed of a great mixture of people, and only in a few cases were related families living in the same village. There had not yet been sufficient time to create new communal feeling, apart from working together on the fields. The following statements reflected the villagers' feelings about the spirit of cooperation: '*Kushirikiana hakuna mpaka wanaeleana*' ('There is no cooperation until they find mutual understanding'), '*Hakuna umoja hata kidogo*' ('There is no unity'), '*Huwezi kwenda kwa mtu mwingine kwa vile ndugu zako hawako*' ('You cannot go to anyone else, because your relatives are not there'). Other such statements were: 'The village has no arrangement to take care of pregnant women', 'When my husband went to the hospital I took care of everything myself, with no help from anyone' (from a mother of eight children). It was also stated that there was no arrangement for loans of money if a death took place in someone's family.

Another indication of the strangeness that villagers felt towards each other was the frequency with which they mentioned the ten-house cell chairman as the person to whom they would go if they had some trouble. In several cases they specified the reason: '*Tulianza kushirikiana lakini hatukufanikiwa*' ('We started cooperation, but without success') and 'Your own relatives are not in the village to help you.' On the other hand, occasions when help *had* been received, either from the village or from neighbours, were also quoted. Individuals helped their fellow village members in building houses by filling the walls with mud. Women had cooperated in beer-brewing and in sewing items for sale, although these activities came to a standstill during the cultivation season.

In general, formally organised cooperative efforts in Mtakuja as in other villages we studied are sensitive to failures. Small discouragements, such as the difficulties with the chicken project, can cast doubts on further attempts and make the village members disinclined to be enthusiastic about cooperative efforts later. Even if women had a fairly good reputation as guardians of common property, slowness to become formally organised was still a noticeable feature in villages during the time of the study. Until that time, the benefits the villagers had gained from living in Mtakuja village came through government services and aid to them, rather than from common production. Generally, the most disheartening of the experiences in a cooperative village is the loss of money and common property. Since individual village members live on the borderline of poverty, they cannot afford experiments which risk the loss of the only surplus they have gathered.

One significant aspect which had changed the status of Mtakuja women as villagers was the fact that both men and women could get a house in the village; it was not only men who could be houseowners, as had been the custom where they had moved from. Eight women from the sample were living in their own houses. The participation of women in the leadership of the village also had a good start. There were five women on the Village Committee representing the various sub-committees (poultry, culture, farmwork, village development). However, there were no women ten-house cell leaders. Of the sample 13 said they were members of the women's organisation, UWT, and 21 claimed to be Party members. At a village meeting attended by the researchers, 30 men and 12 women were present.

The UWT had been more active earlier, but during the cultivation period all common efforts such as gardening, sewing, knitting or learning cooking, which were additions to women's main productive activities, were suspended. Even at other times the enthusiasm for these activities had not been great. Some blamed the leadership, but the main cause was the lack of time, since the women worked full time in support of their families. Thus organising for activities that directly contributed to family income were the only agreeable forms of working whether cooperatively or individually.

The women in Mtakuja had tried to brew beer cooperatively and to hire a pick-up van to take it to the nearby trading centre. This trade was said to have been sabotaged by the beer traders of the sugar plantation and the men in neighbouring Nsyarakia who were losing business: the transporter had refused to continue the business. Another reason for discontinuing the trade was that the profits were minimal.

The women beer sellers were accused by the UWT leader of drinking too freely. This leader was an independent woman with no permanent husband, and it was observed that her status was affected adversely by her irregular marital status — not an unusual divider of opinion among women; married women could have doubts about such women's intentions when they were dealing with men in the course of their work.

The village was registered as a cooperative and every villager was thus registered as a member. Maize and cotton were sold through the cooperative, and the money obtained was distributed at the end of the year to each person according to work done. As a rule, maize from the individual plots was not sold but was used for family food, whereas cotton provided the women with much-needed cash, which was given to the sellers on the spot when the cooperative buyers came to the village to purchase the cotton. Because of the shortage of food and cash, some of the villagers had sold their maize to local traders right after the harvest, when the price was at its lowest. Traders bought a *debe* tin of maize for as little as 3 shillings which they later sold for 40 shillings when the farmers' supplies were exhausted. Beer-brewing, especially during the harvest time, was another reason why there was a maize shortage. Continuing food assistance had encouraged this practice, which probably could have been curbed, at least in part, by offering a better price for the maize produced. Maize turned to beer can turn a handsome profit. Reselling the distributed flour was another reported misuse of food since flour was given on the basis of labour input, regardless of the size or need of the family — thus giving some families a surplus while those with many children did not have enough.

As to the pattern of work, both men and women did weeding during the period of this study, although this is generally considered women's work. Old women were given the special job of pulling out extra seedlings from the cotton and maize, while young girls and boys were assigned to spray insecticide on the cotton. January and February were used for preparing the fields for planting as the rainy season approached. Maize was harvested first (in July–August), and cotton began immediately after. In the months of October–December there was more time for other activities.

If a member of the village died, the surviving partner was allowed to continue to cultivate the plot around the house, although fields further away were returned to the village. If there was a divorce, the partner remaining could continue to cultivate the whole plot and live in the house. A member who moved away but continued to belong to the village could be excused from communal work by paying 250 shillings a year.

Communication in village matters went through the Village Chairman and Village Committee members. It was observed that the announcements were made while work was going on in the fields. National and international issues were communicated to the villagers through eight privately-owned and two village-owned radios, the latter being used in individual houses and not kept available for communal use. No newspapers came to the village except through individual purchases in Moshi town. Educational film-shows were in the weekly programme, but only one film — about spraying insecticides on cotton — was shown during the two-month study period.

Of the skills which the women possessed, beer-brewing was the commonest. Other visible skills were plaiting mats and baskets or doing beadwork. Five of the women were traditional midwives.

It was difficult to assess what prospects the village had of surviving and giving women a place where they could live as responsible ujamaa village members. Here, as elsewhere, much depended on the soundness of the development plans in economic terms and on the villagers' capacity to develop village cooperative activities so that men's labour could also be profitably used for the village's production and not for employment elsewhere. There has been no checking as to whether the husbands who were employed outside the village had in fact paid their dues of 250 shillings since they did not participate in communal labour; the village could have used such income for expanding its productive activities. Kilimanjaro Native Coffee Growers Union (KNCU) had provided the village with shelling machines, and the chickens had been bought with regional development funds which were non-returnable. The next step for the village was to start a cooperative shop. As the village itself had been organised as a cooperative, the members were liable if there should be any loss of money or property.

Mtakuja village suffered from the same faults which have been found in other villages similarly studied: too much of the planning was done outside, and there were too many interruptions such as lorryloads of students visiting the village with minimal work contributions. Yet the necessary inputs — e.g. repair of the water system and improved transport — were missing. The village meetings were for internal planning, but little attention was given to cooperative thinking and sharing of ideas with the officers concerned, and to the making of careful estimates of needs. On the women's side, there was full engagement in the work of the village but far too little educational effort to increase their understanding of factors in production, methods of cultivation and the political principles of ujamaa living. The women's lives were still uncomfortably close to the minimum base. However, it was clear that, despite the drawbacks, the village had offered them the promise of new possibilities in life, and a chance to maintain their families even when they had insufficient support from the fathers of their children.

The two examples given of new development or ujamaa villages, Kilimelile and Mtakuja, are typical of many struggling villages in Tanzania. They illustrate how a new village based on goals for co-operative living can offer women a possibility for economic independence. Whether they ultimately serve this purpose is dependent on the economic viability of the villages in question and on the consistency of the policies of equality in practice. In the case of Mtakuja, it appeared that the external support for building the infrastructure and maintaining the village was not in the right proportion to the village's own productive capacity, with the result that it could not take over the maintenance of the village thus built as if from outside. When the economic benefits that had been promised to encourage people to move into the villages turned out to be economic liabilities, people ended up by cultivating in the area while they continued to live on the mountain or in town.

At the time of our research it was too early to make an overall assessment of life in ujamaa or development villages, but our general view was that it offered the potential for improving women's living conditions.

NOTES

1. 'Orodha ya Watu Wanaokabiliwa na Njaa Wilayani Moshi', 1973/4.
2. For village legislation see Introduction, *Women and Ujamaa Politics*.
3. I took part by visiting families with the students and by contacting the District administration at different times. I was assisted by the KCMC sociologist Ulla-Stina Henricson and an American sociology graduate Mary Zalla, who was living in the area. Each of us had lived in Moshi District for several years.
4. The Mother-Child Health programme is referred to as MCH. Family planning was part of the MCH programme directed from the Kilimanjaro Christian Medical Center (KCMC) in Moshi District. Clinics were held regularly in the villages.
5. In families with greater mobility and higher education the customary practices have less power. The NURU families had had little mobility and their educational level was below average.
6. *Mbege*, a kind of millet used for fermenting *pombe*, has nutritional value even if the basic ingredient, banana, has few nutrients.
7. The Law of Marriage Act, 1971, legislated the establishment of Marriage Conciliatory Boards for settling marital disputes before divorces were granted. In Catholic areas these boards operated under the Catholic Church.

5

WOMEN IN TOWN: EMANCIPATION AND PROLETARISATION

In the urban studies of the 1960s and early 1970s, the town was described as the 'pace-maker' for the wider society, because change proceeds furthest and fastest there and economic and class considerations supersede those of ethnic origin (Southall, 1961, 191–2). This was one of the main reasons why Little considered the 'modern' town as a place *par excellence* for the study of changes in women's status (Little, 1973, 12). Still today, the women's way from the rural areas via smaller towns to large urban centres reflects an important social process in their lives and in the society at large. Changes that have occurred in African societies and in the structure of the cities have, however, made a universal application of a general 'urban model', such as Little suggested, questionable (Epstein, 1972, 246–63 and 263–84).

One of the basic features necessitating a changed 'model' is normalisation of urban life through the establishment of families in towns on a more permanent basis. Thus the transient nature of the residence implied by Little's 'urban model', in which he considered the urban population as being principally composed of 'rural immigrants', no longer holds true. The larger cities as well as the smaller towns of Tanzania already have a basic permanent population of at least two generations of town life. Even if the workers originate in the rural areas, many already consider their residence in the city as permanent.[1] Further, although there are still features which emphasise the heterogeneity of town life, there is at the same time a process of growing homogenisation. People's lives are penetrated by influences which give them common characteristics through their dependence on provided services, their engagement in industry or business, the increasing uniformity of residential structures, and the narrowing scope for ethnically-based cultural activities. However, the growth in the numbers of the working class on the one hand and of bureaucrats on the other accentuates the class base of social life more than in the rural areas, where the kin and cultural structures still prevail over potentially conflicting class interests.

In a country like Tanzania, the adopted policy of national economic planning as a means of bringing about desired social and economic change must also influence the mode of urban analysis. In the process of transformation of the society on socialist lines, the country is restructuring its rural areas. Through legislation, the right of every rural dweller to have a piece of land for cultivation means that potentially it will be easier for the rural women to establish themselves economically in the villages and be the heads of their own households. This reverses some of the earlier processes. Many more divorced or widowed women have been found in urban areas than men in corresponding situations. Whereas among the divorced or widowed male population there was hardly any difference between towns and rural areas, among women the difference was considerable, there being twice as many divorced women in urban areas as in rural areas (Claeson and Egero, 1972, 10).

If the migration to towns has been caused largely by social and economic pressures on the women in their home areas, as is evident from the Bukoba study (see chapter 2), then substantial changes in women's rights to influence their own lives and to hold land in their own name within the new village structure could change the tide.

One of the characteristics of the old 'urban model' was the preponderance of adult males over adult females. The clearest sign of the changing urban pattern is the rapid increase of the numbers of women in towns.

In Dar es Salaam men still considerably outnumber women (by 65,000), which indicates that the urbanisation of women continues to be a gradual process, progressing from smaller centres to the larger ones. In the absence of a detailed analysis of the census figures one can only surmise that the women's movement to towns, besides reflecting the greater permanence of the family in towns, is also a sign of a growing influx of women into the employment sector. It is possible that during and after the acute phase of villagisation (1973–5), many women managed to break loose from the established relationships and sought a way out of the heavy task they would have faced in breaking ground for cultivation in new villages. Obviously the growth is larger in younger age groups than in older ones, since presumably young people have continued to move to towns after finishing their primary school training, as was shown in a child study in 1974 and in a study of school-leavers in the Coast Region in 1973 (Swantz, 1973).

The demographic evidence shows a pattern of gradual moving of increased numbers of women from the rural areas to smaller towns, but it also shows that many men still go alone to the larger towns. The fact that the western Tanzanian towns are more female-dominated than the eastern ones also coincides with the fact that the labour recruitment from areas such as Kigoma has been extensive and the pattern of men going to plantations and industries has been long established.[2]

In the earlier 'model', women's migration to towns could

everywhere be considered as a form of emancipation, even if their status remained low in the town, since they thereby freed themselves from restrictive social ties. Largely because of their inability to hold land, they had been unable to secure maintenance for themselves or their children if they were widowed or divorced without a male off-spring. Becoming a town–dweller may still have elements of liberation for individual women, but new pressures in the changed urban pattern are affecting them in cities too. As the process of industrialisation and diversification of the urban employment structure progresses, inequalities become more pronounced, and the women are being left in a worse position than men. The women are at a great disadvantage in obtaining places of employment. The proletarisation process has also begun to affect women both through their employment in low-income brackets and the low educational levels from which they enter into the competition.

It is significant that although the proportion of women to men is lowest in Moshi town, which has an ethnic majority of Chagga people, for over a decade young single women have far outnumbered older women. This differs from the position in other towns with a different ethnic background, and reflects the difficulty girls have in settling in villages if they have education. A proportionally larger number of girls from Moshi District have obtained secondary school education or even primary education than in other parts of the country. Remaining in the village would mean social pressure to get married, and in that situation the choice of husband is not great. Whereas it is conceivable that a young boy might remain on the home farm and continue to cultivate, it is not feasible that a young girl would stay in her home for long. There is also pressure which is accelerated by economic inflation and the need for increased resources for managing everyday living. Girls become the 'reservoir of disposable persons' (Wright, 1974) who are encouraged to go to town in search of employment, or, failing that, to earn cash or goods in another way. Often not too many questions are asked by the parents about the means of getting them.

The bulk of the female population in small towns, as also in the large cities, is, however, made up of married women living with their husbands. In works on urban women in Africa, an undue emphasis has been placed on the irregularities of marital life and on the women as lovers rather than on their significance as homemakers and educators of their children. The reason for this is that very little has been known of the ordinary women who are often unseen and whose work is considered unproductive from the point of view of the requirements of the nation. Some effort has been made in trying to activate the so-called non-productive sector of the female population in the cities. Characteristically, a news item announced to the public that an eleven-*man* committee had been set up to work out a programme for the activation of women in production in Dar es Salaam (*Standard*, 1973).

The smaller towns offer women greater opportunities for productive activities than do large cities, because women's engagement in agriculture is more easily arranged there. Being able to enjoy the amenities of urban life and to combine that with a productive activity which provides the family with the basic subsistence, food, is an ideal situation from the woman's point of view, especially if the husband would otherwise move elsewhere for a job.

In Iringa a survey was conducted in 1979 during the harvest season, when women who might have been only temporarily living in towns could have been expected to be in their rural homes of origin. The ratio of women was found to be the same as that given in the census figures (Venermo, 1981). It also became evident that most town women were engaged in agricultural activities and found it possible to combine urban life with production of basic foods. This may well be one of the criteria to look for in trying to find the reasons for the differing geographic distribution of female population in towns. However, it is only one factor. The urban centres will need to be analysed in relation to their surrounding areas and their historical and cultural development for factors that have contributed to the specific demographic changes.

From the census figures it is very noticeable that Moshi is the most male-dominated town in the whole country, having 126 men per 100 women. This reflects the local situation both socially and geographically. The town lies so close to the mountain area that it is possible for the family to live on the slopes and take care of the coffee plantation while the husband works in town. The family may even have to have two residences, the husband living in town during the week and going home at the weekends. Although the Chagga men have been the first to go out of their home area for employment, they have been the slowest to take their wives to urban centres. Yet the marriages have been lasting, as has been indicated (see Chapter 3). The combined force of religious and traditional sanctions, and the economic security invested in the inherited coffee *kihamba*, induce the wives obediently to adhere to the duties spelled out in the process of their socialisation.

The women from Bukoba District were the first single larger group of women to leave their rural areas in search of a freer life and better economic opportunities. In Bukoba town the 1967 census showed 119 men per 100 females, whereas 20 years earlier there were 150 per 100 women. Thus, the 1978 figure of 98 men per 100 women in

Bukoba town is not surprising, yet indicates a great change in ten years. In 1957, 71% of all Haya living in Dar es Salaam were women (Hyden, 1968). By 1967 the proportion had dropped to 51%. The Chagga women were only one-third of all the Chagga living in Dar es Salaam in 1967. In 1978 the ethnic group of a person was no longer asked in the census; thus the ethnic breakdown cannot be obtained.

The increase of female population in Bukoba town is not entirely caused by Haya women, who are said to prefer more distant towns with better economic opportunities. That Bukoba town gets some female migrants from Mwanza Region was verified when market women in Bukoba were interviewed by a female student at the end of 1974. Fewer than 20 of the sellers at the market were women, and all of them were from neighbouring ethnic groups, Zinza, Kerewe and some Sukuma. Apart from two couples trading together, the women sellers were not married. The interesting observation was made that these women had acquired knowledge of the Haya language in order that their origin would not become immediately evident. On the other hand, the same student interviewed Haya women at Mwanza market. This is connected with the fact that petty sellers can scarcely make a living from their business and need to supplement it by receiving clients at night. A sense of shame keeps many women from doing this near their home areas.

When women in Bukoba were interviewed for this research, their reasons for coming to town were stated as being partly a desire for self-advancement and partly the difficulty of the situation the women faced in the rural areas. In general, there is a lack of opportunity for a woman to do anything else besides marry, produce and reproduce. Many young women spoke out against marrying and facing the same unhappy situations in which they had seen their mothers. Those with more education wanted to make use of what they had learnt, and they still saw the town as the only place where this could be done. Quite as many were divorced women or widows for whom the town was a refuge.

It is obvious that in regard to the position of women who would want to establish themselves as economically independent individuals, managing their own affairs successfully and living with their children and possibly with some other female relatives, the crucial problem is how they can become respected members of their societies. The problem does not seem to be as difficult in the villages, where they can more easily make living arrangements with their relatives, but there the drawback is the lack of economic independence.

The Haya students doing fieldwork in Bukoba town were of the opinion that without any doubt single uneducated girls living there were commonly considered to be prostitutes, since it is hard to think how else they could manage to survive. In Bukoba town, only girls working in a Church-owned tea house and living in a nearby hostel were classified as not being prostitutes. They were considered more in the category of students who were trying to get on in life. Similarly, in the opinion of the university students, a woman student could live independently and be respected as such.

Most of the single girls were concerned about the right to maternity leave, a right which was later granted by law. On the other hand, private employers had become hesitant about employing girls who were known to live freely thus making themselves liable to become pregnant without any proper arrangement for the care of their children. The same girls who were ready to receive the maternity leave were not prepared to take the man to court for support of their child, for fear of some traditional sanctions which they were afraid would become operative and result in death or illness. The social welfare office in Bukoba also had difficulties in helping young unmarried mothers, because they were willing to reveal the name of the man, but not to start legal proceedings. 'In Bukoba community, women have been brought up to worship men. It is absurd for a woman to take a man to court, especially when they have children together.'

In general, the woman's way to employment in towns is beset by tremendous pressures in the form of sexual harassment. In order to get a job, even a woman with a reasonable education may have to purchase her position by sexual means. Descriptions from offices and other places where women work on the lower salary grades show that women accept money favours from their bosses in exchange for sexual services, in the hope of thus raising their living standards.

Women with little or no education are kept in the lowest employment categories and have almost no say in the work they are doing. Whereas in her rural home a married woman has her own sphere of authority, only in a few higher office posts does a woman gain any sense of being listened to for what she has to say as a person or as a worker. The complete lack of power which most working women experience is partly related to the wider problem of class differences, but is especially pronounced in the case of women. Yet the urban way of life frees women from the pressures of the close-knit rural society and thus at least partly compensates in personal life for what it robs in work life. However, once women no longer have their own personal experience of the restricted past to compare their life with, they will become more dissatisfied with their limited and controlled chances as workers. Thus the liberating function of urban life has its limitations, and as a theoretical model is inadequate.

Women workers in Dar es Salaam

The political, economic and social changes of the last twenty-five years, and especially since Independence, have led to a rapid increase in Dar es Salaam's population, which more than doubled in the ten years between the censuses of 1957 and 1967.

The gap in the sex ratio has gradually been closing. In 1967 there were 123 males per 100 females, whereas in 1957 there had been 131 and in 1948 141. In the 1978 census the difference had narrowed to 115 males per 100 females. Women's migration to the urban centres has a pattern of its own, which differs from the migration pattern of men. Men migrated first to the city on a temporary basis, leaving their wives at home to till the soil. They formed temporary relationships with the local women and with women who had themselves migrated to the town independently. With the stabilisation and improvement of employment conditions, it eventually became possible for the up-country man to take his wife to town to live there on a more permanent basis. Thus the female population of Dar es Salaam consists of at least three major groups:

1. The local women, who have been born and raised in the city.
2. Wives of migrants, whose number has increased in recent years with the more permanent nature of employment and better living conditions for families.
3. Single women — unmarried, divorced or widowed — who come with the specific purpose of finding employment.

The conditions and interests of women, as well as their reasons for being in the city, differ according to the group to which they belong. The women who have grown up in Dar es Salaam or in the Coast Region have had relatively easy access to their rural areas of origin. Many cultivate in the valleys around the city or periodically return to their rural homes, especially for the rice-growing season. They have never changed their semi-rural pattern of life and they keep it up through their annual visit home.

Contrary to what one would expect, one does not find a large number of employed women among this coastal group which has had the longest residence in the city. One reason for this is their close contact with the rural areas. Another is the low level of basic formal education on the coast. This has prevented the coastal women from looking for jobs. Furthermore, in the coastal family pattern a married woman is secluded by her husband and must not appear alone in public places. She is prevented from venturing out to become a market seller or from finding more formal employment.

In a survey of civil servants in two government ministries in Dar es Salaam, it was shown that very few wives of those in the lower income groups were engaged in agricultural activities or were self-employed. In one ministry, 2% of the wives were self-employed and 3% engaged in farming and in another the figures were 3% and 1% respectively.[3] Of these wives 20–23% had no education.

The survey also showed that the number of economically active wives was less than half in the highest income group and less than one-third among those on the minimum salary. Two-thirds of the employed wives had been trained as nurses/midwives, but only a little over one-third of these were using their education. Two-thirds of the wives trained in education were employed as teachers. The largest group of wives who were engaged in some form of economic activity had husbands in the income bracket of 855–1,420 shillings.[4]

A survey conducted by the Sociology Department of the University of Dar es Salaam in 1970 showed that in a random sample of 169 wives in various areas of Dar es Salaam only six were self-employed, fourteen cultivated a *shamba* and fifteen were wage-employed.

A growing number of city women have a backyard garden plot which may bring financial returns.[5] Some of these women act as self-employed sellers of small garden produce or home-made baked goods. A number of women are engaged in poultry-keeping on a commercial basis. They have all had some initial capital to invest and are often wives from the higher-income groups. As more and more houses are being built on the outskirts of the city, so more women have the opportunity to cultivate a garden, bringing in income as well as aiding their own subsistence.

In spite of increasing opportunities for employment or self-employment, the city woman is relatively inactive. This is a complete contrast to the overworked rural woman who, despite her heavy workload, is the most important person in the system of production (Boserup, 1970). The domestic work involved in bringing up a family in the city at the present time, however, requires a lot of organisation and thought in order to manage on the available income. So to call the city woman idle is not always justified. The difficulty of arranging for the care of small children would make large-scale employment of married women impracticable at the moment, even if the opportunities were there.

The married city women also have other difficulties to cope with, partly caused by their social and economic isolation. Marriages become individualised unions losing earlier kinship connotations. Divorces become common, leaving women without a husband's support. Since employment is hard to find, such women look for new alliances with men who may welcome a temporary city companion or who otherwise are ready for a change. Many of the low-income employees in this study were in this position. Their initial social mobility made it possible for them to come out of the domestic sphere and look for an independent income.

However, the majority of city women continue to be engaged in the everyday drudgery of maintaining the present male labour force and caring for the growing generation. Living in the heart of crowded urban quarters, these women paradoxically become isolated socially and economically. Their important rural roles are, in the city, limited to the sphere of an individual household and they are fully dependent on their husbands for support. When this support becomes insufficient, or fails completely, such women look for paid employment. However, the scarcity of jobs is very discouraging. Relatively few women succeed in getting work through the employment agency. New migrants who have the time and energy to look for work are more likely to succeed there than are older residents, although the latter may, on the other hand, have more working relatives and friends in the city, who can inform them of openings.

The Dar es Salaam urban woman's economic inactivity is in contrast to what happened during the early stages of the Industrial Revolution in Britain when women and children made up the bulk of the labour force. When colonialism introduced wage labour in Tanganyika, men were recruited. The lengthy period of capitalist social welfare ethics shielded women from forms of direct exploitation under colonial rule. Instead, their labour was mobilised to produce cash-crops and food to support the labour force on plantations and in urban centres, through customary agricultural production. Not until after Independence in 1962, when minimum wage legislation was passed, lifting the very low level of wages geared for the maintenance of the individual labourer to an amount sufficient to cover the living costs of his wife and family, did women begin migrating to the towns in substantial numbers to follow their husbands. Having been the mainstay of agricultural production in the rural areas, women were relegated to an inactive, unproductive existence in the city. Their labour resources remained untapped, job opportunities were restricted by an underdeveloped industry which has persisted to the present day.

In 1967 the industrial sector (manufacturing) accounted for only 1.6 per cent of total employment (*1967 Census*, Vol. II, 142), but since then industrialisation has been more rapid. In the 1978 census the urban centres accounted for 13 per cent of the total population, but some of the industries are scattered in rural areas. Unlike the early stages of the Industrial Revolution, factories today do not generally rely on a heavy input of labour. An exception to this was the Urafiki textile factory, studied for this research. It had been built

by the Chinese on labour-intensive principles. The effect of techno-
logical transfers from the West is generally to structure industry on
the basis of current standards of capitalist efficiency and automa-
tion, with the result that a very competitive job market ensues.

Women composed only one-tenth of the total economically active
population in Dar es Salaam, according to the 1967 census. Num-
bering 10,398, they were distributed in the following sectors: services, 24%; clerical, 20%; mining, communications and labour,
17%; professional and administrative, 17%; agriculture, 15%; and
sales, 7%.[6]

The historical preference for male labourers still prevails in current hiring practices. In a survey of seven large towns in Tanzania,
including Dar es Salaam, the unemployment rate among women
(20%) was over three times higher than that of men (6%) in 1971
(Sabot, 1974, 8). One-quarter of women migrants arriving in the city
during 1966–7 were still looking for work in 1971, in comparison to
only 1% of the men (*ibid.*, 10). The women's lack of skills and education doomed them from the outset. Three-quarters of all unemployed women had no job experience, as compared with half of the
unemployed men (*ibid.*, 17), and 48% had had no training, while
only 19% of the men fitted that category (*ibid.*, 19).

The study on female employment

The forces militating against female employment appear formi-
dable. Who are the women who succeed in securing work? Focusing
on the low-income workers, a study was made of women workers in
Dar es Salaam. The aim was to discover what factors led these
women to seek urban employment and whether there were any
attitudinal changes in women after securing a job.

The degree of economic independence *vis-à-vis* husbands, lovers
and/or relatives resulting from women's minimum-wage earnings
was another point of interest, as was also how women workers
managed to cope with both job and home responsibilities. In all, did
employment improve the quality of a woman's life and lift her status
in her own eyes and in the eyes of others?

The research method and sample

With official permission, low-income female workers were
approached while at work in the Tanita and Urafiki factories during
March–July 1973, and at the Ministry of Education, the Prime
Minister's Office, and the University of Dar es Salaam during the

months of April–July 1974. There was also contact with a sample of self-employed women who were mainly vendors in Msasani and Kijitonyama peri-urban areas. Sample sizes varied: Tanita workers, 150; Urafiki workers, 63; women cleaners at the Ministries and University, 46; and women vendors, 36.

Four female university students talked with the women mainly at their places of work. The research students were encouraged to adapt their methods to the particular work environment and to participate in the women's working lives to the greatest extent possible. As a result, at the Tanita factory the researcher worked in the various sections of production, talking to women workers and later writing up on a questionnaire general information about their age, education, marital status, children and employment. At the Urafiki factory, information was sought and recorded in the same way, but the more technical nature of the work did not allow the interviewer to participate in production.

At the Ministries and the University more detailed interviews were conducted, aimed at uncovering the motivation and social pressures experienced by women workers. The student researchers taught literacy classes, which gave them the opportunity to hear women's attitudes on various subjects, and the women wrote down answers to the questions as a writing (and thinking) exercise to the extent that they were able. The potential of this kind of learning situation for the political or social analysis of a given situation became obvious. The women were motivated to talk about their lives and their difficulties, and to take a more active part in the advancement of their social and educational level.

The Tanita, Urafiki and cleaners samples were supplemented by information gathered from visits to individual women workers' homes.

Information from the women sellers was obtained through conversation and informal interviewing while the women were at their stalls. They were asked about their motivation for going into private business, the relative financing arrangements, and about their families and education.

(a) *Tanita factory — unskilled labourers.* Tanita, a parastatal company operated by the Tanganyika-Italian company and located approximately 3 miles south-west of Dar es Salaam city centre, employed 1,260 workers for the processing of cashew nuts for export.[7] Female employees (900) vastly outnumbered men. This was attributable to the unskilled nature of the work, where lack of training or of previous job experience was not a hindrance. With practice, sufficient dexterity and speed could be achieved to meet the required work quotas in the time allocated. A sexual division of labour existed between the various sections of the factory. Men were assigned to the storage areas and washing and roasting sections, because these involved carrying heavy loads or were otherwise hazardous to health. Only women were found in the shelling section, grading department and packing section. Both men and women worked in the shaker group, dry room and peeling section.

In the shelling section, the women's task consisted of inserting nuts into a simple machine which cuts the nuts in half. This was exacting work and entailed considerable discomfort. The workers' bare hands were exposed to corrosive acid from the nuts, and sores resulted. Hence women in this section were paid slightly more than workers in other sections of the factory, but the terms of employment placed women in an uncertain position. Hiring was only on a temporary basis to begin with — one-third of the 150 interviewed were working on temporary terms — and only after workers had proved their ability were they hired permanently. The trial period could last three years. Meanwhile, workers could be dismissed at any time for failure to finish the daily quota (women running behind schedule gave up their half-hour snack break), for eating or stealing cashew nuts, poor-quality work or irregular attendance. The section operated on two shifts, and only permanent employees worked on the night shift. City buses were reserved for their transportation home late at night.

Workers were provided with a first-aid station under the auspices of the Dar es Salaam Occupational Health Services. At the time of the survey, there was no canteen. During their half-hour break women ate packed lunches or bought fruit from local vendors. Child care facilities were not provided at the factory. Working mothers who were interviewed felt that a day care centre located at the factory would be inconvenient, because of the problems of transporting children from distant parts of the city.

(b) *Urafiki factory* — *skilled and unskilled labourers and clerks.* The Urafiki textile mill began operating in 1969. At the time of the survey it had built up a capacity to produce about 22 million metres of cloth annually. Production was highly labour-intensive. The factory employed 4,443 workers (Dec. 1973) on a three-shift rotation system.[8] Women numbered 371; the bulk of those interviewed were involved in the production processes, which included carding, setting spindles, operating spinning machines, weaving, dyeing, printing, engraving and inspection. Women were also found in the clerical section, sales and marketing, the design department, the dispensary and the canteen; a few were in management, and six ex-National Service women[9] were employed as guards. Only jobs which could be injurious to health, e.g. carrying heavy loads or working in the cotton-grading area where cotton dust could cause respiratory diseases, were not assigned to women. During pregnancy, close to the time of delivery, women could be shifted from strenuous work and from night shifts if they so desired.

The employment of women had been a matter of contention. Because of the inconvenience of maternity leaves and the special arrangements with shifts, the management made a decision to stop hiring women. The Party intervened and the idea was abandoned. Yet forbidding preferential hiring practices did not rectify the structural discrimination against women which is built into the society as a whole, in that fewer girls are competing on the Standard 7 level which Urafiki hiring policy demanded. In 1971 girls leaving Standard 7 were only 34% of the total in Tanzania (Development Plan 1971, 9). Furthermore, for married women the night shifts conflicted with home responsibilities. The persistence of traditional cultural values deprived the women of husbands' help with household chores and child care. Women without such obstacles were able to distinguish themselves. One example was a woman working in the machine workshop, having received training in mechanical engineering while doing National Service.

Women were free to seek any vacancy that arose at the factory. If they felt discriminated against, the matter was referred to an Employment Committee.

The Urafiki factory was noteworthy for its welfare services. There was a canteen providing subsidised meals, a cooperative shop, living quarters for 500 families, and a kindergarten, which greatly eased the domestic responsibilities of the working women. A literacy programme was underway, with the active participation of women.

(*c*) *Ministries and parastatals — women cleaners.* Research which combined statistics on the job ranking of employees at three government ministries showed that out of 923 employees, 233 were women (Lindberg, 1974). Women were more heavily weighted at the bottom of the pay scale; a quarter of the women employees were minimum-wage earners, working as cleaners or messengers, whereas fewer than one-fifth of the male employees fell into that category.

The Prime Minister's Office and the University had workers' canteens. Day care services for children did not exist at any of the three locations.

(*d*) *Self-employment.* Self-employed women are found throughout the low-income housing areas of Dar es Salaam. The sample was drawn from those in Msasani and Kijitonyama peri-urban areas, north of Dar es Salaam. Four-fifths of the thirty-six women sold food items: rice and beans, buns, vegetables, fruit, coconuts, *togwa* (local unfermented beer), porridge, fish and tea.

Most women traded throughout the year. Vegetables were seasonal and those selling them switched to buns for the rest of the year. In two cases women were involved in merely selling the surplus from their *shamba* or in selling as a pastime. They restricted themselves to the season of their product.

2 tailors and 2 bar-keepers were also interviewed.

Some findings from the survey

Background and material conditions. The women in the sample ranged in age from 16 years to over 50. 44 different ethnic groups were represented, of which coastal Zaramo women were the most numerous — 53 of the total 279 interviewed. In analysing the ethnic composition of the sample, one could see that from those areas which traditionally seclude women within the home the number of employed women was relatively small considering that they lie close to Dar es Salaam. On the other hand, areas in the south from which men had historically left the villages to work on plantations were rather well represented. There, women had been forced to handle matters which would not normally fall to them. Differing educational patterns in various areas also had a differential effect in the sample; the Chagga, Pare and Hehe, for example, used their higher educational level to advantage in the skilled work at Urafiki.

Two-thirds of the women in the factory samples said that their parents were farmers. The one-third which came from other sectors is a larger proportion than the non-farming sector in the total population. Among the cleaners, a surprisingly large number — one third — said that their fathers had died, while 5 had deceased mothers. Most women said they helped to support parents.

The level of education varied between places of work. The average number of years spent in school was, for the Urafiki workers, 5–6; in the Tanita group it was less than 3, and among the cleaners less than 2. Of the 46 cleaners, 10 said they had no primary school education and 13 refrained from answering, which indicates that they too had none. Reasons given for not attending school were that there was no school in their home area while they were growing up, or, more commonly, that their parents could not afford the school fees. Despite this, in many cases their brothers had been sent to school. Only 3 cleaners reported completing Standard 7.

With regard to education outside the formal school system, only 10% of the women workers said they had attended Koran School. Informal education of an unspecified nature was mentioned by one-quarter of the factory workers, which probably meant that they had taken part in organised adult education at one time or another.

All of the women cleaners had attended adult education classes for varying lengths of time. The women were interviewed in the context of their adult education classes, which gives a certain bias to the information.

The vast majority of the women interviewed were immigrants to Dar es Salaam, hailing from all parts of Tanzania. Of the respondents 15% were born in the city. The immigrant workers among the cleaners had resided in Dar es Salaam longer than the others, on average close to 10 years, while the immigrant Urafiki workers' residence had been less than 6 years. In any case, women's employment in sectors other than those requiring higher education is mainly a post-Independence phenomenon.

The mean average commuting distance to work from the place of residence was 2.8 miles.[10] Two-thirds of the Tanita women relied on buses, the rest walked; on average they spent 1.3 hours each day commuting. Of the Urafiki workers 60% used buses, 19% rode in vans and 21% walked. They spent close to an hour in transit daily.

The majority of women were living in rented accomodation: 19% of those at Tanita, 13% at Urafiki and 9% among the cleaners owned their own homes jointly with their husbands. Two-thirds of the women working at Urafiki and Tanita paid between 25 and 49 shillings rent per month for a one-room or two-room arrangement. Cooking was done outside, in areas used in common with neighbours. Toilets were also shared.

Focusing on the family arrangements among the cleaners, in a few cases relatives were occupying adjoining rented rooms. Of the divorcees 40% said they lived alone in their rooms: only four reported living with a male friend. It became evident that divorcees and single women were reluctant to reveal that they were living with men or having them pay their rent, yet this seemed to be a common practice. All ten married women lived with their children and their husbands, who in most cases paid the rent, although one woman said she shared this expense with her husband. In most though not all cases, slightly better material conditions were detected for married women compared with divorcees, based on the fact that the majority of the married women had piped water and electricity.

The marital status of the women interviewed varied significantly among their respective places of work, and this sample of women workers did not adhere to the average marital pattern of Dar es

Salaam's female population.

In all four samples divorcees were more numerous than in the census figures (average 19.4% as against 8.2%). This correlates with Westergaard's (1970, 16) survey of female employment in Dar es Salaam, which found that 41% of the female heads of household sampled had wage employment compared with 9% of the married women whose husbands were the heads of households..

Comparison with the census figures also revealed that at Urafiki and among the cleaners there was a far lower proportion of women living alone for their age brackets. This adds further evidence to the theory that the primary job seekers in the urban female population are women shouldering family responsibilities without a husband's financial support.

The average number of children per woman worker was: 2.1 among the self-employed; 2.0 at Tanita; 1.8 at the Ministries and 0.8 at Urafiki. When comparing the survey figures with the mean number according to the census, in three out of the four samples the women workers bore fewer children. Fertility rates are in general depressed in urban areas relative to rural areas (Claeson and Egero, 1972, 20). This can be attributed to a number of factors:

1. greater access to birth control (Urafiki was note-worthy. The dispensary offered contraceptives to women after the birth of their first child);

2. a large proportion of divorced women in the population (which is accentuated in our selective survey of women workers);

3. higher rates of infertility, related to the higher divorce rate; infertility as the cause for seeking employment;

4. a probable catalytic cause or effect of female employment outside the home. However, this requires further research to validate.

Are women with fewer children freer to seek employment? From the answers pertaining to marital status, it would seem that the motivating factor in securing a job is the woman's degree of economic independence, which could operate regardless of the number of children. Fewer children might, however, indicate the widening of women workers' interests in matters outside the home, causing a reduction in the emphasis on childbearing.

Arrangements for the care of young children during working hours did not show a clear pattern. The majority of the cleaners had a woman relative, usually the woman's mother, helping with the pre-school children. One married woman and one divorcee reported paying a person for child care. Seven sent their children home to their mothers in the rural areas, where their upkeep could be partly absorbed by the children themselves. There children are useful, performing tasks like scaring birds from crops, herding, and so on.

In general, however, the mother of young children is expected to contribute to their upkeep.

At Tanita, reliance on the grandmother was not prevalent. Representing a fairly local Zaramo population, other younger family members — usually sisters — were immediately at hand, whereas a quarter resorted to hiring helpers.

At Urafiki, the sample was stratified to illuminate differences between the child care practices of unskilled wage earners and those with higher earnings. Surprisingly, the minimum-wage earners hired helpers in almost three times as many cases. The high-wage earners' sample is smaller, with a greater likelihood of being unrepresentative. Nevertheless, the discrepancy may be partly explained by the greater representation of younger relatives, whose help may in the long run prove to be more expensive than hiring a helper because it generally involves taking them on as dependent members of the household. The difference may also reflect a greater consciousness of money values among those who 'hired' help even though the actual arrangement may have been the same in both cases.

Work arrangement and finances

(a) *Wage earners.* All but one of the women interviewed at Tanita were minimum-wage earners. 7 of the 150 were daily labourers being paid 11 shillings per day. The University and PMO cleaners, unlike the Ministry of Education cleaners, were interviewed after the wage rise of May 1974, with the result that many stated salaries of 340 shillings — which had been raised from the minimum wage of 270 shillings. Only 3 cleaners and 11 workers at Urafiki earned more than 400 shillings and none at Tanita were on this level.

Of the 42 and 22 women who reported their husbands' income level at Tanita and Urafiki respectively, over two-thirds stated that their husbands earned 400 shillings or less. 9 of the Tanita workers had unemployed husbands.

In the sample of cleaners almost nobody reported having other forms of income besides their salary and that of their husbands. Only one woman said she received foodstuffs from her family. Not one had her own garden, since there was no room for cultivation in the places where they lived in the city.

When the respondents had relatives working in town, there was never any mention of their helping financially, except with loans, because they had their own families to feed. About half of the cleaners said that they were compelled to borrow money in certain months, usually from neighbours. Those at the University often asked for advances on their salaries. Of the cleaners 43% mentioned sending money home to their parents, some only when they received a letter asking for it but others as a matter of course every month. Supporting parents seemed to be such an unquestionable duty that when one woman was asked why her salary was spent on her child and parents, and none went to help her husband with household expenses, she retorted, 'What if I had no job? He [the husband] would be in a worse position, helping my parents as well.'

It appeared that the women did not consciously plan the use of their wages. When the cleaners were questioned on this subject, many said there was no way they could know how much they spent on food each month, because they bought it day by day. During the study the prices of staple foods were rising, which brought further complications in making estimates of food expenditure. As for clothes, most women said they could afford perhaps two dresses or two pairs of *khanga* clothes in a year. Thus they spent about 60–100 shillings annually on their own clothes, and if they had children the expenditure was much more.

Apart from the monthly rent bill, water — if they had a tap, as about one-third of the cleaners said they did — usually cost about ten shillings. Those who took water from a public tap paid nothing or paid 15–20 cents per can. 11 paid 5–10 shillings monthly for electricity.

Most of the women, especially those with children, considered that they could not afford to pay for entertainment such as the cinema, football games and dances. There were exceptions, especially among the single, who used their salaries for incidentals and said that they often went to the cinema. A few married women went to the cinema with their husbands. Of the divorcees, the younger ones went to dances when taken out by men.

Bus fares were an additional daily expense. Not only money but time was spent waiting as long as an hour for the bus. To ensure getting to work on time, women woke up between 5 and 6 a.m. and one related how she rose at 4 a.m. towards the end of the month, '*mwezi kona*' ('when the end of the month is just around the corner'), when she could no longer afford the bus fare and had to walk to work.

When the cleaners were questioned concerning previous work experience, it was found that in the majority of cases (72%) their current job was their first salaried employment. Those with previous jobs had worked as child nurses, house servants, bun or *maandazi* (doughnut) sellers, and factory employees.

Most women had had to keep up a persistent search for the jobs they now held. Some had looked for over a year, writing many letters of application to various places. Only one said that a relative had helped her to find a job. Another said she had 'slipped in through the back door', meaning she had appealed to some man's favour. Judging from the wide representation of tribes, nepotism did not play a prominent role in hiring.

(*b*) *Self-employed*. Nearly half the self-employed women were motivated to work by financial necessity. Of the women interviewed 28% stated that they initiated their business in order to earn extra spending money to supplement their husband's income. On the other hand, 5 out of the 36 were under compulsion to trade by either their husbands or brothers. In most cases the women lacked marketable skills. Trading in foodstuffs near or at their homes was a feasible job solution.

In most cases profits were small. Two-thirds of the women reported purchasing food ingredients and/or fruit and vegetables wholesale, which they in turn sold; 9 avoided the role of middle-woman by selling items from their own *shambas*. Daily returns ranged on average from 3–10 shillings. There were of course exceptions. One woman boasted that her husband's wages were nothing in comparison with the thriving business she had in selling tea, *maandazi*, coconuts, rice and beans. With a confident and independent air, she declared: 'Whether he [her husband] is at home or with other women outside, I don't care. I have my own money and the house is mine.' She was saving to buy a beer store.

The two tailors represented another class of women. Sewing machines had required a considerable outlay of money, which one had got from her husband and the other, who came from South Africa, had accumulated after her divorce. Her 6 children lived with their father.

The bar-keepers earned a substantial income, which enabled one to send 100 shillings home every other month. The other said her salary adequately covered rent, electricity and water bills, and clothing for herself and two children. One rented a house from the National Housing Corporation, the other owned a car. In both cases, their living quarters were attached to their beer shops.

Of the respondents 16 said they were self-supporting, while 20 were working out of necessity. A quarter were dependent on their husbands, 5 relied on their brothers and sons; 5 considered themselves jointly responsible, along with their husbands, for their family and business finances. One woman described herself as self-supporting, but said she welcomed 'contributions' for the financing of her beer shop. She stated that within 6 months her 'contributors' received the amount they invested with accumulated interest.

The division of profits varied: 70% of the women were free to dispose of their returns in the manner they deemed fit, 3 decided with their husbands how the money was to be spent, but on the other hand, 6 were forced to hand over the cash to their husbands (4) or brothers (2). It is interesting to note that those brothers who helped finance their sisters' businesses demanded all the returns, whereas of the financier husbands (totalling a quarter), only half appropriated the surplus. The 3 sons who helped finance their mothers never claimed any of the returns.

Why women migrate seeking urban employment

The Dar es Salaam survey showed that women from areas with a history of male labour migration were more likely to migrate to the city than those whose societies had remained more insulated from the cash nexus and which consequently held more traditional social attitudes towards women.

Women's departures were not characterised by the rebel's desire to flee familiarity and embark on a new and different life. The decision to move was not even a sharply defined independent action. Members of the extended family were present in the process of migration to shield the women from culture shock. Out of 174 respondents, 96% stated that they were accompanied or met by a relative when they came to the city; their brothers were most often mentioned. Although some came specifically to seek work, others had arrived with the intention of visiting relatives living in Dar es Salaam. Only later did they decide to stay on. Housing did not seem to be a problem on arrival; there was always some family member who preceded them, with accommodation to offer before they made arrangements for themselves. This is not peculiar to women. Sabot (1974, 11) reported that three-quarters of all male migrants receive assistance from relatives or friends during the early stage of their stay in the city.

The majority of women in the sample were between 16 and 24 years old when they arrived in Dar es Salaam. The mean age was approximately 22. Conducive ethnic social patterns seemed to be a necessary pre-condition for migration, but events experienced by the women as individuals, reinforced by social pressures within the village, provided the final impetus for the actual move. Personal hardships for the women in their societies centred around the incidence of divorce and/or the death of a parent, which appeared to be the two primary causes of migration.

It has already been pointed out that the urban rate of divorced women is twice that of the rural, whereas there is no difference for divorced or widowed males. This proves that above and beyond the town's unstable atmosphere for conjugal relationships, which leads to a high divorce rate, a selective influx of divorced women is present. Of 43 cleaners who described what their marital status was when they had arrived in Dar es Salaam, over half said they were divorced at that time (9 were married and came with their husbands, 8 were single and one was widowed). Moving to town is a considerable step for divorced women, especially those aged over 30, of whom there were 3. Nevertheless, the risk is not unjustified. A divorced woman's position in a village is precarious, as has already been demonstrated. With no guaranteed rights to land or to the proceeds from land, it is understandable that it is divorced women in particular who look for employment in town.

The death of a parent, especially the father, throws responsibility on the adult offspring to ensure the economic wellbeing of the widowed parent. Filial duty is strong and daughters as well as sons are solicited for support by their parents. The education of children is often viewed as an investment, and if daughters are educated, parents expect returns from it. If the wife earns money herself she is free to send it, and in general it is considered her duty, which is intensified in the event of the death of one or other of her parents. At the same time, the actual responsibility of supporting parents is very seldom expected to be the sole duty of a daughter, whereas the same cannot be said for a son; he cannot excuse himself easily from this duty. Not surprisingly, therefore, the women who did not answer the question as to whether they supported their parents all had brothers.

An interesting fact to note is that among the cleaners only four women out of 31 who responded were the first-born in their families. In the majority of cases it was one of the younger sisters who left for employment in town. Knowing the traditional family patterns in many parts of rural Tanzania, one assumes that this fact is significant. From the point of view of continuity in the family line and traditional custom, it is most important that the eldest daughter receives treatment which is in accordance with the family custom. For example, among the Zaramo the first-born child's initiation or puberty rituals are most elaborate, and adherence to the prescribed pattern is of greater concern to the parents than in the case of later-born children.[11] It may well be that allowing other daughters to go and try their luck in town is a case of making the best of both worlds. On the other hand, many of the women who came to Dar es Salaam had already been married before arrival (four-fifths of the cleaners in the sample), and thus the authority of their own parents over them would not be the same as over someone coming straight from her parental home. Yet the sense of responsibility for support does indicate that the tie persists.

Underlying traditional customs and personal circumstances leading to women's migration to the city is the impelling promise of a less exhausting and less materially deprived life than that of a peasant woman. The perpetual toil on the fields and with the domestic chores, where daily food had always to be made by going through all the preparation processes from the ground to the cooking pot, is changed to purchasing food items. Social pressure to bear many children, as was the case in the extended family setting of the village, slackens. But the city is by no means a panacea for women. The socio-economic contradictions of underdevelopment operating in an urban context perpetuate inequalities in the sexual division of labour under a different form.

New social contradictions

Questions were put forward to probe the women's views about the difference between town and country life. The change was conceptualised primarily in material terms. Women were in general agreement that work pressure was reduced in town, even though they had jobs. Village cultivation was described as very hard, sweaty work with long hours. In the city, on the other hand, they reacted against having to buy everything, even water. The majority had no plans to return to their village to stay. However, women were in the habit of returning home annually in their three-week paid vacation.

The serenity and good neighbourliness of village life was missed. Some remarks centred on relationships with women living in the same yards. More than one said that urban women lacked the spirit of cooperation that existed among women in the village. One woman expressed it as 'Town women are selfish'. Another related that she could not leave a pot of boiling meat for more than a minute for fear that another woman in the kitchen compound would steal it — the non-working women envied her for the more expensive food she could afford. She said they spread rumours that she cooked delicious food in order to take their men away from them ('*Anapika vizuri, atuchukulie waume zetu*').

Nonetheless, visits to the respondents' homes revealed in most cases a very close relationship with a select circle of women neighbours, which has probably developed over the hours spent together cooking, tending children and plaiting each other's hair in the crowded quarters of their residences. When the interviewers arrived at the women workers' homes, their hostesses always insisted on introducing them to their close neighbours. It was observed on one occasion in Kariakoo that the women practised female solidarity in an extreme form. Seated as a group at the entrance to a courtyard, plaiting one another's hair, profuse greetings met the occasional woman passing through the courtyard, whereas if a man passed, not only was he not greeted but often the conversation would stop and everyone would eye him with suspicion. Indeed there was a strictly delineated division between men's and women's social worlds, not unlike that which exists in the rural areas. Guests were not shared in common. When a man invited his friends to his home, the wife served them food and drink quietly. She was not usually encouraged to join in their conversation. The wife's visitors, on the other hand, were almost ignored by the man. With such social ostracism of women by men, it is not surprising to find that women prefer to share their leisure time with other women. Inevitably, then, their deepest thoughts and feelings come to be voiced only among themselves. They come to believe that women have different minds and emotions from men — and that they will get understanding only from other women.

Work: the awakening of consciousness

The unskilled, routine nature of their jobs allowed women workers little pride or enthusiasm for the work itself. Among the cleaners no-one had any suggestions for further improving or systematizing their work. One woman said that she just followed what her supervisors directed her to do 'like a flag following the wind' ('*mimi ni bendera nafuata upepo*'). Another woman cynically asked: 'Why should I think of the impossible? Do you think if I give an idea the boss will agree? After all, we don't participate in any decision-making meetings. The top people don't expect any reasonable suggestions from a cleaner.'

The wage differentials existing at their workplaces helped to create class consciousness among them. They did not indulge in fanciful dreams about material wealth unavailable to them, but many entertained feeble hopes of improving their status in life through promotion. Learning to read or speak English was considered the means to gain promotion, and this the cleaners determinedly set about. All viewed differences in education as the reason for the social gap between the *wakubwa*, big people, and themselves, the low rank, *kima cha chini*. One old woman, in response to a question about why she ran away from school in her youth, confessed: 'Ah, my friend, had I known that education would be of such use, I would have gone on with it.' Others, more resigned, recognised that it was too late for them to benefit to any great degree materially from studying, yet they were eager to learn. There was more than one case in which a woman said that she received letters from her children in school but was unable to read them; she would be satisfied if only she could read those letters. Workers' education classes were therefore embraced with enthusiasm. Those held during working hours were all attended at the Ministries, the University and Urafiki. Tanita workers complained that they were too tired to go to classes after work, and had family commitments which hindered their participation. Observations at the Ministries and the University revealed various levels of success, contingent on a number of problems: lack of books; lack of a definite course structure, arising from the absence of regular teachers; students of widely varying reading ability being forced to amalgamate under one teacher; and beginners not being taught to read phonetically, but merely memorising words on the page.

Women workers as yet have not involved themselves in political activity as a means of putting forward their specific demands. Two-thirds at both Tanita and the Ministries and 18% at Urafiki were TANU Party members. Yet when the cleaners were asked if they spoke up at meetings they all said they preferred just to listen. They were still inhibited by centuries of customary deference towards men. UWT, the women's organisation of the Party, would seem to be the organ through which their voices could be heard. 12 of the 46 cleaners said they were UWT members.

The question of what activities UWT engaged in at their place of work revealed an orientation directed at the encouragement of domestic arts and/or entrepreneurship. At the Ministry of Education, one of the women who said she was very active in the organisation stated that they sewed, knitted and cooked. At the University, most of the women were not members but mentioned that UWT raised money for the nursery school in the area and had sales. At the Prime Minister's Office, there was special mention of making and selling table-cloths and baskets. But there were several other answers. 2 women said they did not know what activities UWT was involved in. Another 3 said: 'It brought progress to the nation', and 2 others said it did nothing. One woman, a divorcee, explained at length why she was not interested in joining UWT. 'The leaders do not like single women, only those who are married. The UWT members are the greatest gossipers among the women. They always talk about their husbands and the single girls.' Underlying the petty jealousies over husbands is the fact that the uneducated women's social status is determined by whom they marry. In 1967, 80% of the total female population had had no education, and only 6% had completed schooling above Standard 4 (*1967 Census*, Vol. VI, 124).

Wives of men in government and parastatal posts, many of whom have risen from the ranks of the peasantry, have new-found class interests tied up with their marriages. They are without land as an income base, and would have no means to keep their children. Unlike women workers, divorce is undergone at very high cost; hence, the fear of losing their husbands, which the above respondent mocked, has an economic basis and cannot be looked upon only at the level of personal feelings.

Work and marriage: the appearance of notions of sexual equality

The significance of wage employment *vis-à-vis* sexual equality struck a few of those interviewed. One woman observed: 'A woman can have the same job as a man if she has qualifications — you see, both men and women are cleaners', but she recognised that this is not enough to earn women social respect. 'On the other hand, the relationship is not very smooth because men despise and ridicule women very much.' It was when she was derided by men that she saw the 'importance of having a husband, because it is not often that a married woman is ridiculed.'

Attitudes towards men seemed to be moulded by marital status, and the married women seemed to accept the *status quo*. However, one of the oldest women, who had been married to the same husband for many years, recognised the reality of the situation. 'Being a woman is punishment because, first of all, we are considered very weak physically compared to men. We cannot decide on our own unless we seek the advice of men. Men consider women as equal to children in thinking capacity. As a woman, I cannot build my own house, because men will ridicule me. It is not proper for a woman to have her own house. She has to be in either her husband's, her father's or her brother's house.'

Those who were single did not usually express very strong opinions concerning their relationships with men. Although wary of the lack of trust between the sexes, they all desired to get married and have children (only 0.2% of the female population of 45 years and over had never married, according to the *1967 Census* Vol. VI, 251). The woman in the survey who had the most education, a Form IV leaver, had very definite opinions of marriage. She thought that the relationship between men and women had been spoiled because these days so many young people embark on marriage 'as a lark' and in this way marriages do not last more than two to four years. Replying to the question about what she felt she could expect from her husband-to-be and *vice versa*, her views were distinctively set apart from the others. There was no mention of obedience to a husband, or cooking and cleaning for him, but instead she gave an answer full of romantic hopes. 'I will love and care for my husband through happiness and sorrow and I will depend on him to do the same for me.'

On the other hand, militant refusal to remarry was voiced by some of the divorcees. Many had consciously rejected their socially-ascribed role of legitimate dependence on men, and were of the opinion that the best thing to do was to live with a man without marrying him, which avoided many problems because both could go their own way when they wanted.

Women workers could be generally characterised as independent women, who may rely on men-friends to pay their rent and on members of the extended family to look after their children, but who ultimately depend on their own capabilities and determination to earn a living.

The degree of economic independence attained by working women

Women's economic independence hinges on their marital status in conjunction with their ability to earn a steady income through wage- or self-employment.

Married women's earnings appeared to be of secondary importance in relation to those of their husbands (except in the case of the married women interviewed who had unemployed husbands). However, in many cases the money income did help to enhance their social position *vis-à-vis* their husbands, being pooled with the head of the household's wage to pay domestic expenses or used to buy things for themselves and their children that perhaps could not have been afforded otherwise.

Single workers without dependants had the luxury of indulging themselves on a modest scale. The wages of divorcees and widows, on the other hand, were usually stretched to support dependants. Employment figures reveal the imperative of a money income for unattached women. In Sabot's survey the figures for those registered as looking for work were lowest among the divorcees/separated/widowed, at 20% of their total, as opposed to 31% for unmarried women and 40% for married women (Sabot, 1974, 4). Sabot has interpreted this as meaning not that divorced women are less desirous of jobs but the opposite; divorcees are forced to secure jobs as soon as possible, often settling for lower incomes in order to avoid having to return to the countryside. In contrast, married women can take their time in selecting a job that suits them, relying on their husband's wages in the interim. Single girls likewise can usually fall back on parents' or relatives' support while holding out for better opportunities.

Interviews revealed a growing consciousness of the economic and social advantages of gainful employment, which correlates with Sabot's findings (*ibid.*, 8) that between 1965 and 1971 the women's unemployment rate, excluding subsistence-income earners, increased from 7% to 20%, whereas the men's unemployment rate decreased from 7% to 6%. Many of the women in the sample stated that they knew of women in their neighbourhood who were unsuccessfully looking for work. They themselves spent months applying at various places, spending much more time than men in job-hunting (*ibid.*, 10). The median average was three years compared to the one year of men. Given the extremely competitive job market, those women who fail to secure wage employment accommodate themselves in a variety of ways, according to their degree of economic need.

1. Some — usually divorcees who have no relatives to rely on in the town — are forced to return to their home area.

2. Other women resort to prostitution. Divorcees with no other means of income are the most likely to do this, as described elsewhere. Women's dependence on men is implicit in the economic order as it still operates. Only a few very determined, uncompromising divorcees manage to escape subservience to men in a domestic household set-up.

3. Some women can contribute to the family income in non-financial ways. Sabot (1974, 6) reported 14% of the urban women in Tanzania as falling into this category, producing baskets and handicrafts for use in the home and/or engaging in agricultural production for home consumption. Married women are most commonly found in this group. Their activities only supplement the family income. Ultimately they are dependent on their husbands. In recent years, the number of women has grown in towns where women can without too much hardship engage in agricultural activities.

4. Self-employed women engaged in marketing home-made goods for sale are again usually married. Sabot (*ibid.*, 47) noted that 28% of all 'non-wage earners' are women, but they are weighted in the low-income yielding activities, i.e. street trading and farming (*ibid.*, 75). Nevertheless, self-employment depending on the initiative of the individual can make possible considerable financial accumulation and business expansion. Bar-ownership generally seems to be the target of successful women entrepreneurs and to afford them positions of economic independence and power.

The problems defined

Structurally, the underdeveloped economy is not geared to involve women workers, who are nonetheless encouraged through the mass media to engage in productive work outside the home. Job opportunities are not sufficient in quantity, nor are adequate social welfare provisions made to allow women to leave their children during the day. Moves by UWT to ensure equality in work opportunities for women were earlier aimed at high-level positions (*Daily News*: 'Women can take up any job — UWT', 4 June 1975, and 'Women, men to be treated equally in job promotion', 23 April 1975), whereas more recently greater efforts have been made to extend day-care facilities to all income levels. More difficult to grapple with is the problem of women's mass unemployment, which hinges upon their unequal access to the job market.

The World Conference of the International Women's Year adopted in July 1975 the 'Declaration of Mexico', which stated: 'The issue of inequality as it affects the vast majority of the women of the world is closely linked with the problem of under-development, which exists as a result not only of unsuitable internal structures but also of a profoundly unjust world economic system.' The mid-term women's World Conference in 1980 reiterated in strong terms the call for justice within the world order. Stunted industrial growth and consequent restricted job availability have been the root cause of women's limited opportunities for economic participation in urban areas, and hence their continued weak and dependent position in society. Increased emphasis on industrial development within the Tanzanian economy has created new employment opportunities for women, but the structural and attitudinal bias against women has not thereby been rectified.

First TANU, later CCM, Party documents, and government legislation have attempted to ease women's vulnerability on the urban job market in Tanzania. TANU principles formulated in 1967 directed that the government should give equal opportunity to men and women irrespective of race, tribe, religion or status. But women's lack of education and training and their liability to become pregnant tend to mean economic losses to private and government corporations and agencies, making them reluctant to take steps to open jobs for women.

Only 14% of those completing Form IV in state schools were girls. At the same level in private schools girls accounted for 49% of the total. This would indicate that if the system of allotting fewer places in secondary schools to girls did not operate to exclude girls from the state school system, many more would take advantage of furthering their education. As it was at the time of the study, only those whose relatives could afford the fees were able to continue. Consequently, girls entered the job market with lower qualifications, pointing to the need to rectify sexual discrimination in the society at a stage much earlier than the actual hiring.

The Maternity Leave Act of 1975 was a positive step providing all women workers, regardless of marital status, with three months' paid maternity leave. But as Boserup (1970, 113) points out, in underdeveloped countries where the birth-rate is high, paid maternity leave legislation may lead some employers deliberately to avoid hiring women. She suggests that maternity leave should become a social responsibility whereby the government deducts funds from all employers, whether or not they employ women. This is suggestive of a general policy stand that could operate advantageously regarding women's employment whereby the benefits of women's social labour in childbirth and in housekeeping could be distributed in the family and through the society at large. In turn, an attempt could be made to distribute the costs in like manner.

Another major problem area is the difficulty of combining home responsibilities with wage employment. The self-employed women using their home as a base for their business (with clearly-defined workload and hours) can quite easily combine the two. Women with salaried employment find it much more difficult. When they return home from work, household tasks require their attention until they retire for the night. Even more perplexing is the child-care problem. Very few factories or workplaces have provided day-care facilities, with the exception of Urafiki. Women generally work out their own solutions depending on their family circumstances and financial position. The survey revealed that:

1. An older relative, usually the grandmother, was most frequently (41%) left in charge of pre-school children. This seemed the best solution, involving a mature person, who could better ensure their safety and who was usually not a great drain on the family income, because she was either fully independent or only semi-dependent. In the latter case, if the grandmother was involved, traditional responsibility towards the aged was accorded while easing the family's needs.

2. 28% of the respondents hired a helper. Wages, when mentioned, ranged between 40 and 75 shillings per month, a considerable amount of money for women themselves receiving only minimum wages. Yet hired helpers were more prevalent amongst lower-income groups, as previously observed.

3. 19% of the women in the sample left their children in the care of a younger relative. This situation arose when no older relative was

available. It often entailed sending for the adolescent from upcountry, whose food and lodging then became entirely the responsibility of the recipient family. MacRae (1974, 47) observed this practice among working university graduate women. She pointed out the heavy social costs involved. Young girls often no older than twelve or thirteen were deprived of primary and secondary school education.

4. Women were also found (6%) to use their own older children to look after the pre-school ones. Although this may seem a logical solution it nevertheless has the same great social costs as in the case of using other relatives. In both cases a more detailed study of the exact arrangements made for these adolescents, and what the effect of universal primary education has been on child care practices amongst women workers, is necessary.

5. Another 6% of the women had made arrangements with neighbours. No details were given concerning payments or other forms of reciprocity. It appears to be a promising solution for the future if neighbourhoods can be organized to provide a reliable day care service under the supervision of older women or those who prefer not to work outside their home. But it requires sufficient trust among the women to allow their children to be left in the care of people who are not their kin.

The problem of child care is the key to urban women's involvement in production. The establishment of day-care centres (or night-care for those working late shifts) at the factories or in local neighbourhoods is essential. In addition, campaigns to politicise men to shoulder equal responsibility with their wives in household duties are a vital adjunct to women's active participation in production outside the home, which the country has called for. Women are being burdened with responsibilities for which the social situation has not yet matured. On the other hand, with social changes more and more women — and families — are in a position where the employment of both single and married women is an economic necessity. The society must carry the cost of this through improved services.

NOTES

1. Information from a survey made by Sandberg about the Rufiji in Dar es Salaam.
2. E.g. in the 1978 census, the ratio of males per 100 females was in Musoma 95, Kigoma 96, Iringa 99, Sumbwawanga 100, Tanga 111, Dar es Salaam 116, Arusha 120, Moshi 126.

3. Data from a survey conducted by Professor Olof Lindberg, BRALUP, 1974.
4. The minimum salary after the raise was to be 380 shillings.
5. In 1975, with the government's emphasis on *Kilimo cha Kufa na Kupona* (agriculture for survival), there was a marked increase in the agricultural activities of city people. Continuing shortages of food supplies have increased the numbers engaged in farming, including people from the higher-income bracket.
6. At the time of writing, the detailed breakdown of economic data from the 1978 census was not yet available.
7. Due to the nature of cashew nut production, Tanita is an exception to the general choice of capital-intensive techniques in Tanzanian industry, although relative to other methods of processing cashew nuts the 'oil bath' method employed at Tanita is fairly mechanised.
8. Urafiki provides an exceptional example of a labour-intensive factory in relation to Tanzanian industry as a whole, as well as within the textile industry. The original labour/capital ratio was five times that of a capital–intensive textile mill in Mwanza.
9. National Service is combined work and military service, compulsory for all young people, men and women, who complete some form of higher education.
10. Rough estimate calculated from most frequent locations stated.
11. The maturity rites of the first-born are significant in the life-cycle of the mother, and thus cannot easily be neglected, any more than the obligations laid on her afterwards through marriage and bridewealth.

6

EMERGENCE OF WOMEN AS LEADERS

This has been a difficult chapter to write, because the life stories of women who have become the leading characters in the building of the independent nation of Tanzania are so close to me, both emotionally and in time. I have followed their lives as co-workers and friends, rejoiced with them over their personal successes, and followed their children's progress and sometimes failures in school and in society. But I have also grieved inwardly — not openly with them, for they have never asked for pity. The dignity and understanding with which they have borne their lot and risen above their personal pain and worry have never ceased to amaze me. A chapter such as this should be written by someone further away from the scene.

However, a change in generations is occurring. A new generation of young women is growing up in cities, filling offices and other workplaces. They no longer share the struggle of the pioneers, yet in many ways they become victims of the men's world, the values of which they wake up to after harsh experiences. The years of youthful attraction are short; many are left alone with their children to fight their way through life, and they take full responsibility for the upbringing of their children. A woman who has established herself in some profession, or has a fairly secure employment, generally prefers to stay alone and keep the income for herself and her family rather than take a man whom she would then have to serve, in addition to her other duties. 'I rather stay alone than join a man — it is a burden rather than a help' is something I have heard repeated numerous times.

When writing about women as leaders I have chosen to write first about the generation of women who are the mothers of the present women leaders on the national level. I shall then relate this to the beginnings of the UWT — *Umoja wa Wanawake wa Tanzania*, the Union of Tanzanian Women·— and its role in leading the nation's women.

Women's unknown history

Several books have been written recounting the life stories of the pioneering men in the history of Tanzania. In these books women have been conspicuous by their absence. Yet today's women leaders have been preceded by generations of women who prepared the way for them, and whose lives form an important part of the nation's development.

153

Mama Salome — I shall refer to her as Foibe — belonged to the first group of women who, from their youth, were taught the Christian faith in the Pare mountains. Until her fifteenth year she called herself '*mswahili*', meaning a Muslim, but in that year, at midnight on Christmas Eve, she attended a service which impressed her. She wanted to know more about its meaning.

I was drawn by the preaching and the singing. I said to myself, 'This I will follow.' I went to my elder sister and told her, 'There is a true God and He looks after His people.' I went to my father who did not follow any religion. He had two wives. I said to him, 'I go to school.' My elder sister said the same to him. My mother was very pleased when she heard this. She advised us to go to father very gently. He was drinking his beer and we again said to him, 'We are going to school.' It was our elder brother who then helped us to get the permission. When father refused, the brother encouraged us. He himself went to father persuading him, 'Let them go to read.' And so it was. We went for six months after which we came to father again. 'We want to be taught for baptism.' We were then taught Christianity for two years: Old and New Testament, Cachecism, preparation for baptism. I learned to fear the Ten Commandments. If you break one you have broken them all. We read in Usangi for two weeks, for the third we went to Shigatini where the missionary lived and we attended the services. The missionary was our friend. He came to our home. We ate together. . . . The missionary died in 1934.

Christian men wanted to marry Christian women. Otherwise there was trouble in the home. When they were about 25 years old they had to build a house for themselves before they could marry. The missionary did not want them to bring a wife to their fathers' home. My father did not care. For him the main thing was that he would get wealth by marrying me off quickly. My brother stopped him, and all of us, both mothers included, were baptised; only father remained outside.

Before I was married I was among the six girls who were sent to Old Moshi, Kidia, to a girls' school where Mama Elisabeth, another German missionary and a Chagga man were teachers. We learned among other things cultivation, cooking, sewing clothes and choir. My husband-to-be went to Marangu for teacher training. We were married. My husband was a good man. We had nine children whom he loved much. We set aside money from his salary to enlarge the house we had built and cultivated to feed the family. He was a man of God. I stayed here when he went for upgrading and later to teach in Ashira. But he worked too hard and got ill. He wrote down his testament. Everything was to be left for me — the house, the cattle and the money in the bank. Not even the children were mentioned so that his relatives could not claim any of it on their behalf as would have been the custom without the testament. We had bought this land. Had it been inherited land, there would have been trouble. It was a day of great sorrow when my husband fell down and died.

I was left with nine children, the youngest not yet two years old. I went to ask for some help from the mission that had employed my husband. I was told that the salary ends the very month when the person dies. That day I cried, oh, how I cried. But I thanked God that I was not left pregnant, that I had all my strength left. Not once did I say 'I shall die.' My cries I cried to God alone. I remembered the children and cried, 'These children will be like cattle, or they will go to cultivate fields for others. And how their father loved them.'

My husband's brother came from time to time and wanted to marry me. He knew I had money in the bank, because according to custom I had to state before the relatives what the deceased had left behind. The brother was married and had his children. Why would I have gone to look for trouble? He came and banged on the door. But there was nothing he could do. The statement of his brother was clear, 'What I leave belongs to my wife.' The brother tried to lure me to do business with that money. In the end he did not even greet me any more.

I had got used to taking care of money already before my husband died. He brought the money home and put it on the table. We divided it together: this for a loan, this for food, this for the bank. God's word had really done work in him. He did not touch drink. First the salary was 25 shillings; when we had three or four children it was 30, one more child and it went up to 50. People said 'Those people have money.' It was not much but we could buy mattresses for the children to sleep on. After the teachers complained that their wages were too small, they were paid according to their years of service. We were then able to enlarge the house. Had he died before we did this, we would have had trouble; the children could not have continued in school. Then what would have life been for them!

My mother had been skilful in cultivation. My only way was to cultivate. One year we harvested much, another year not so much, but always we had our food and some to sell. It is not me, but God who has helped me to stay well. We ate and sold beans and maize. Banana we grew, cows we milked. Money we used for buying meat, clothes and school fees. We have built more buildings after the children have grown older.

And so, together with the eldest daughter who became a community development worker and never married, Foibe cared for her family. Rising long before dawn, she walked down the mountain to cultivate on the plains. And then taking with her a load of firewood, or grass for the cattle, she returned to take care of the home chores. At times she had to walk for hours and hours to reach the Education Office in the nearest town to beg to be excused the school fees, especially when the children reached the age to go to secondary school. 'What made it possible for you to go on through it all' I asked her. 'Could any woman have done it?'

Everyone lives in her own home in her own way. There would have been those who would have said, 'I cannot do it.' Men tell me, 'You have been created like a man.' It's a gift, not my own doing. If you tell yourself you can, why could you not do it? If they tell me, 'A man could do it', why could I not do it? Have I not been created equal to a man? We may have been created weaker in our body, but our head thinks as well as man's head. And even my body — have I not carried loads like no man — eight sacks of rice up from the plains? Only we women carry such loads.

If you set yourself to do something you will do it. But now I am getting old and cannot do as much any more. But neither can the men of my age, we all grow weaker. These days men cultivate more, but this head has carried more. Every day, going down and coming up. I washed clothes for children, I hung them up for the night from the ceiling. Not once were the children sent home from school for having dirty clothes.

If the house is yours, you have no problems. Others who were not Christians were married to the house of the husband's father. There is much trouble when the husband dies. The widow might be given a small house to use if the father-in-law or brother-in-law has the means for it. But a hut is not a house, and there is nothing but trouble. Just as I order around in this house, so that even my married daughters have to listen to me here, so would it be if my daughter should marry and move into a house in her in-laws' compound. She would have to listen to her mother-in-law. If then the husband dies, she has nothing to say. I could do as I wanted. If I earned one hundred, I set aside fifty; if fifty, I set aside twenty-five. We could have a feast at Christmas; I have had clothes to give my children; if they went on a safari I have had some money to give them. The *shamba* they shall divide between themselves.

The Pare women patiently bear up, but they really suffer; you do not understand how much they need to endure. Where would they go? These days people are much more superficial, and they break up their marriages. My children had school friends who said, 'What's the difference? Your father has died, but I have not seen my father for the whole term. My mother gives me the things I need. When I go home my father is gone. He never comes home until we have gone to sleep. In the morning when I wake up I don't see him. Father is like a leopard to me. Only mother is with us children.'

Foibe brought up her nine children, giving each of them a good education. The two youngest daughters have master's degrees from the university and are on the staff there. Of her son, Foibe had this to say:

My son is building a house below the hill. He lives in Dar es Salaam and has entrusted the building arrangements to me. He sends the money to me, and I write it down. I order the supplies needed for building. I know the prices. I have a plan which the builders follow. I pay them for their work.

I have never needed to buy clothes. My children and children's friends whom I have cared for have sent to me what I have needed. I never have needed to beg for anything. Food I have here, bananas and potatoes I dig from around the house. Maize I buy and I milk the cow.

Mama Salome always has some grandchildren staying with her for whom she cooks and cares; they also help her in little chores and keep her company so that she never needs to feel alone. All her children are working in different parts of the country, but their home of origin in Usangi is the kind of foundation for their lives that could hardly be bettered. The university-trained daughters are the first generation in public leadership, but it is only when the nature of their background is known that the sources of their creative work can be appreciated.

Mama Judith — Judith's mother — from Kagera (Bukoba) Region had a different story. She too had been left alone to manage with three children, not because her husband had died, but because, like so many others in her area, she had been divorced by him. The social system put no obligation on her husband to provide for his family; research showed that the husband could either insist on keeping the children himself, or he could let them stay with the mother if that was what he found convenient. If the mother wanted to hold on to her children, she could not afford to start even customary proceedings for fear of being separated from them.

Mama Judith was determined to make the best of her situation. She had no way other than to set herself on the edge of her brother's *shamba*, where her labour was made use of and she herself felt very unwanted. She worked for hire: with the small children she grew bananas and time and again little Judith carried a heavy bunch of bananas on her head for sale as she walked to school. Gradually the money she collected in this way became sufficient for buying her own plot of land. Only then could the family feel safe, knowing that no one could claim the land on the grounds that it was part of the male right of inheritance within the husband's or her own kingroup.

Judith's mother was determined that her two daughters and her youngest child, a son, would get a good education. Like so many other women in her area who also supported their children's education, she could have said it was not her responsibility, and that the man should do his duty. However, a mother's desire to educate her children arises from something deeper than a list of duties prescribed in customary law. One can of course put it down to her anticipation that at some future time her children would be able to support her if they attained high places. But the road was long and stony and required many years of hard toil, self-denial and belief that education was an investment that paid dividends — in itself evidence of women's conscious share in the national process.

Judith became a teacher. After a study tour abroad she became headmistress of a church school for girls. She married an engineer, but continued her work. Her brother graduated from the University and entered government service. Judith provided strong leadership in her society and church. I saw her leading a women's study programme and chairing a seminar, and no man questioned her right to leadership: not even when she was strongly critical of the way men were using their power in church and society. Her own personal experience of this gave depth to her analysis.

An example from an area where women's attitudes have been considered conservative has been given in the context of Rufiji. A male student there too told how it was his mother who had encouraged him and his brother to go on with their studies until both graduated from the University (cf. the story of Maimuna Saidi). One does not have to search far to hear stories of the respect of sons for their mothers. This respect is part of the reason why men admit, albeit very reluctantly, that the position of women in their society is not what it should be. They have genuine respect for their mothers, and perhaps even their sisters, and like to look at the total situation in that light.

I consider life-stories such as these very significant when one evaluates the contribution of women to the national life. On the other hand, has the potential leadership and experience of women that lies hidden in every village been encouraged, and utilised, and if not, why not? If there has been some conflict in trying to create a strong women's organisation, it should also be seen as a generational problem, and not only as evidence of class struggle or as élitism versus ordinary peasant women. The younger educated women have tended not to have sufficient respect for the work of their mothers. Modernisation has been too overpowering for the young women to be able to look at their own personal and cultural inheritance from such close range and draw from its rich creative resources. There has been an obvious difficulty in building on the work of the village women and accepting their leadership on their own conditions and on the basis of their particular strength.

The question of how the women's national organisation, the UWT, was formed and how it functions still deserves attention here, and we consider the difficulties experienced in making it truly belong to the women themselves in the light of what has been said above.

Organised for what?

Before any national efforts were made to organise women, individual women — as we have seen above — showed their great strength within their families, churches and communities, in which they exercised their qualities of leadership. Their stamina and endurance were possible because of their basic vitality and faith in life. The fact that in women's development there is generational continuity, with one generation building on the work of the previous one, was not given conscious recognition when UWT was set up. The break with the past has been overemphasised by thinking of women as an ignorant, backward part of population, as targets and not actors and initiators in development. However, women's role in political mobilisation preceded that of mobilising them for development. In the effort to get the women's votes, they were not regarded as 'ignorant'. There Bibi Titi's leadership and women's support were recognised. Only after Independence did the problem of how to organise the women arise.

In July 1962 women from all parts of Africa gathered in Dar es Salaam to attend the constitutional Congress of the All African Women's Conference. The delegates from francophone Africa had an air of sophistication with its roots in Paris, which showed itself not only in their speeches but also in their style of dressing. But the self-taught, forceful character of the leader of the Tanzanian women's organisation then in formation (she was in the Chair) probably represented better the prototype of the African women who were to emerge. They, like her, were going to be self-made women, the first to shoulder the responsibility for the political and socio-economic liberation of the independent countries and the emancipation and rehabilitation of women, so that they could 'participate in all creative activities in the social and political fields of Africa' (Draft Constitution of the All African Women's Conference 1962). In Tanzania they had been recruited in great numbers for the struggle for *Uhuru*, independence. But the political fervour prevailing at the time of their recruitment in support of TANU no longer existed when the women's national organisation was inaugurated several years later.

Umoja wa Wanawake wa Tanzania, UWT was officially inaugurated soon after the All Africa Women's Congress, its purpose being to unite the existing women's organisations and form an umbrella for them. Only officially registered bodies were recognised, which meant that most groups, especially those belonging to religious communities, remained outside, although the latter had played and continued to play an important role in training women for local leadership. In many places they have worked closely together with UWT and have provided capable leaders.

The Ministry of Cooperative and Community Development, with the help of foreign advisers, made the draft constitution for the National Women's Organisation in Tanganyika, which was to take the place of the former Tanganyika Council of Women, TCW, the President of which at the time was Maria Nyerere. At a preparatory meeting held in July 1962 to discuss the draft, only representatives from the TCW and YWCA (Young Women's Christian Association) were present, together with the male officers from the Ministry, one of them an expatriate. It led to the actual founding of the organisation in the following September, after the All Africa Women's Congress.

It was overlooked at the time that women in villages and in the towns had their own forms of association not recorded anywhere, and the services of the natural leaders of the social groups within the local structures were not asked for when the new structures were being created. These groups included women's local credit associations on the coast, dance societies across tribal borders in Dar es Salaam, loose associations of instructresses of young girls, adepts of ritual cult groups, informal social and religious groups of mutual support, and age and neighbourhood groups for mutual aid in work and in the preparation of feasts and funerals. Thus an opportunity to build on women's ways of linking up and acting together was missed. This meant also that women's own needs for meeting together were not considered when the activity list of the new association was planned, and that the capabilities of women leaders in the preceding social organisation were not consciously incorporated. These are fundamental reasons for the difficulties the UWT has encountered in trying to bring the ordinary women into the local branches as active members, or even to arouse their interest. Although UWT soon became known all over the country because its structure closely followed that of TANU with its local branches and representatives at all administrative levels, the question of leadership and the actual working out of the programmes on a regular basis have caused constant struggles. The reasons for this, I suggest, go deeper than the class conflict between the educated women and the non-educated village and town women. Women's organisation did not grow straight out of the political participation of the women in the struggle for independence, nor did it incorporate those who had already learned something of the art of leadership within their own sphere of activity. When during our various studies ordinary women in villages and workplaces were questioned about the significance of UWT to them, their answers almost invariably had the tone, 'We have not yet come so far.'

There were of course leaders who came forward. The role of the religious women's organisations in this connection has already been mentioned. One brief lifestory exemplifies what, in spite of the difficulties, could be repeated a hundred times with only slight variations. Cases of active Muslim women have been described in earlier chapters. For many individual women, the political and women's organisations have had great significance, even if their mass influence and problems in creating a wider base are open to criticism.

The 60-year-old Mama Mhingo tells of her life:

I am married and have nine children. I have had three husbands and have been with the present one for 35 years. As the last child in my family and being a girl, I had no school education. My father took me out after one week of school. But I tried to learn to read and write on my own. It was also my own initiative that I became a Christian at the age of 13 years. It took one year to be baptised. When I got married I was chosen as a leader of the youth group of that time, because my first husband was a church leader. His Christian life influenced me. But he died after two years of marriage.

In 1957 I took adult classes and I did so well that I was chosen to teach others. I taught for two years, especially home economics according to my standard. I was also good at singing and I taught others to sing.

I then joined TANU. Shortly afterwards I was chosen to represent my people in the District Council and Regional Council. I also represented the women in the women's regional council. I attended many seminars. Presently I am the Chairperson of UWT; I have held the responsibility since 1962. I have written many political songs. I have tried to unite women of different faiths. When we are visited by guests, I gather together all women regardless of their faith. So I am able to combine the political and church activities because each does help the other.

Mwalimu Nyerere means a lot to me. He advocates emancipation of women, the thing Jesus did. Because of Nyerere I am free to speak. His thinking of equality of all people is wonderful. He is helping the poor as does the Bible tell us. He wants all people to be free. [Information from Bukoba provided by Bengt Sundkler.]

The new women's movement took its pattern at first from a Western concept of what a women's organisation should be, but it was later changed to follow the Party organisation more closely and to give it support. In many cases, what UWT was to do was formulated by men. Sewing, cooking and child care, useful and necessary as they were, were the arts in which men wanted women to be versed, at the expense of economic and educational activities which would have broadened their horizon and given them independent sources of income. However, the women have gradually taken the direction fully into their own hands, and have changed the programme so that it does consist of economic activities. There has been much pressure on them, because the village governments have often assumed that women's activities form a cooperative way of earning money for village funds, while men's cooperatives have taken it for granted that the participants are the main beneficiaries. Yet time and again I have come across women's cooperative groups operating solely for corporate purposes and leaving the women without any personal compensation for their labour. However, wherever active UWT branches are found, they are those in which women share in the income from cooperative shops, bars, or hotels. The women's own basic need has been to supplement their means for the subsistence of their families, for which they carry the main responsibility.

The 1980s has seen a new vitality in regard to women's place in the society. Already in the 1970s, the national organisation from time to time led demonstrations for political or women's causes (e.g. against polygamy) on the streets of Dar es Salaam. These often occurred spontaneously, and drew together urban women from different sectors. Women have become more outspoken in claiming the rights which the policy of the Party prescribes for them. For this they have needed women leaders versed in legal and public affairs, as well as those who in their personal lives have dared to go their own way, regardless of social pressures.

Whether women have become leaders or not has not in general been determined on the basis of their husband's status, although this criticism has sometimes been levelled at UWT by outside commentators. The level of women's education has not always been comparable to that of their husbands. In the early stages of girls' education it was common for a man to avoid marrying an educated girl, for fear that she would make demands that he could not meet, or simply that he would not be able to remain lord of his house as he envisaged a man to be. It could not be relied upon that a male leader's wife would become the leader of women in a community. A wealthy man could treat his wife or wives as a way of demonstrating his wealth, by amassing for her piles of *khanga* and *kitenge* cloths and jewellery and, more recently, by supplying the home with fridges, radios and a car. At the same time, he might shield his wife from exposure to the public eye for fear that her privileges would attract other men. It has not been uncommon for men to prevent their wives from taking up leadership.

Women's leadership has emerged among women who have had to take matters into their own hands after becoming widows or divorcees, or otherwise being independent. As indicated earlier, more often than not the chairpersons of UWT and those chosen to represent a community in meetings and conferences at District and Regional level are of the class of independent women who possess the necessary freedom of action. The second category of women who have taken over leadership is that of primary school teachers, if they work in their own home areas; this happens less often if the educated women, whether teachers, nurses or clerks, are working outside their home areas.

It is significant that the national elections for UWT leadership were delayed in 1978 because of the lack of candidates who would run for the local leadership positions. I was working with a group of educated women in a large coastal village at the time of those elections. To an outsider, it seemed that an artificial tension was created between the ordinary peasant women and the educated women over the question of leadership. The educated women hesitated to stand for election, because in political speeches so much emphasis had been laid on leadership coming from the people themselves. Fear of forming an élite class also prevented them from starting a local study group for furthering their own political and general education. Apart from the fact that the existing social leadership was ignored, there was another reason for a seeming gap between the two groups of women: the way the girls are brought up. Boys are socialised for public life from the beginning; they are free to move about in public places, and are not prevented from 'hanging around' where people of all backgrounds meet and talk. While still young, they are given tasks of public negotiating if their kin relations demand it. They run errands and learn the skills of peddling. The social world of men is more variegated and complex from the very start than the world to which the girls are socialised. Girls' verbal skills are often trained only in close woman-to-woman communication, and consequently the distances between different ethnic groups and shades of culture may form a more significant gap for women than for men. Women in their homes can seldom be contacted directly; the mediation of men is necessary, which makes it even more difficult for women from another ethnic group to approach them.

In their own environment, the women have no difficulty in appearing in public in front of hundreds of people. They plan and execute their own rituals, their work and what they earn. But they are restricted by taboos as to what they can and cannot do — and as to the way they must conduct themselves in the presence of other categories of people, men or women. On the other hand, women who find their way through these obstacles are versatile and capable leaders who speak eloquently and offer concrete assistance to one another across the borders.

Climbing the ladder

The Tanzanian woman has taken her place in society in an increasing variety of roles. The higher managerial posts are, with a few exceptions, still reserved for men, but the number of women in the lower ones has been growing. In 1974, there were an estimated 9,300 (2%) women managers at various levels (MacRae, 8).

Academically trained women form a category of their own. According to MacRae, women who had completed their university education had not suffered much discrimination on the job market.

Women who carry the responsibility of training institutes, districts, divisions and wards have earned the respect of their male colleagues, their students, and of citizens in general. Here we see a radical change in attitudes. The simultaneous resistance toward the advancement of women and the proud acceptance of it is one of the strange paradoxes that are to be found within a society undergoing rapid and radical change. The experience of the parents who have discovered that their wage-earning daughters are more faithful in supporting them than their sons compares with that of the citizens who are surprised to discover how efficient and diligent their female administrators are. The women will have to redeem their right to leading positions through service of high quality, even when they have to do it while bearing a double load of duties. On this score their less educated relatives lighten their load, but may do so at the expense of their own personal progress. We should seek to analyse the social cost of the advances which some members of society make so that a growing inequality does not grow up as a result.

The overall development that I have witnessed as a participant during the more than thirty years that I have been associating with Tanzanian women is astounding. Much of it is still hidden from public view but it has matured quietly among women high and low. The quality of conduct in planning and decision-making, in conceptualising and in carrying out plans is demonstrated both domestically and in the wider political, economic and social context. What is still needed is a greater awareness of it among the women themselves and in their society at large.

7

CONCLUSION: THE WOMEN'S ROAD AHEAD

In the elections held in the autumn of 1980 only one woman candidate was elected to Parliament from the constituencies. Another thirteen were chosen in the first session of the Parliament as regional members or as representatives of such bodies as the women's organisation UWT.

The decline in numbers of women representatives (from seventeen to fourteen) can be interpreted as a reflection of a loss of interest in keeping up the push that the Women's International Year in 1975 gave to women, a trend prevalent also in other parts of the world. Changes in the woman's position can be measured in one way by women's increased share in public life. The emphasis in this book, however, has been on another measure: what effects has development had on the rural and urban women at the lowest end of the social scale.

The chapters in this book have given some aspects of the historical background to the position of women in Tanzania today. They have also illuminated the prevailing social order and its possibilities to accommodate improvement of the women's lot. Not much has been said about the educated women. The focus has been on the rural sector and the lowest-paid workers in towns. However, the so-called 'élite' women have been in many ways pioneers, and much has been expected of them.

The role that the Christian Churches have played in bringing up an educated, mature and responsible class of women leaders has been mentioned only in passing. The school system, inadequate as it was, still gave hundreds of women the foundation from which they have been able to enter into public life. Many have become teachers, nurses, policewomen, clerks, and so on, besides being wives and mothers. They have brought up large families from which new leaders have emerged. The respect in which men hold their mothers is often a reflection of the support they have received from them.

The question is whether the new generation of women will be better equipped to take up leadership in society as well as playing their role in their homes. Will women continue to be treated as an inferior sex which needs to be especially allowed for, for the sake of equality, or will they be respected for what they are and what they can accomplish?

The core of the problem is in the issue of power and the means of power, of which the right to land has been the most important. The women can contribute fully to village life only when they can speak as people who determine the use of the output of their work and whose access to land is equal to that enjoyed by men. In the cities, women's independent income already gives them a chance to build their own houses (already at the end of the 1960s 18% of Dar es Salaam houses were owned by women) and to start their own businesses. It is only a matter of time until it inevitably happens that women will take over sectors of trade, for example the banana trade in Moshi District or poultry products in Dar es Salaam. However, a woman's gaining of economic power almost invariably causes a problem in the balance of power within the domestic unit. That is the main reason why the male population wants to prevent women from gaining, in practice, the equal rights that all in principle affirm.

Can women gain equality and respect in society without a breakdown of the family institution? The conclusions from the individual studies of this book indicate that women have two possibilities between which they often have to choose. They may have been driven into a position in which they subject themselves to continued hardships and physical and mental suffering. They are overburdened and not given much scope or opportunity for determining their own preferences or prerogatives. This state of affairs is the most convenient one for the society at large; the women in that position are the easiest to manage, and for this reason large sections of the male and even the female population advocate the ideology of the woman's obedience to the man as the divine order.

The other possibility is for women to take matters into their own hands and play the power game with those who wield the power — whether men or women. In general terms, women are as competent as men at this game, as the women who have risen to the top positions in their nations have demonstrated. There are women in Tanzania who are demonstrating it also in lesser positions. However, neither of these alternatives is satisfactory. Is there another option?

In general, women are not prepared to play an open game of power. Much of the current discussion and writing on women's issues in the world concentrates on the question of how the world order could be changed so that reason and common sense would gain ascendancy in the concern for human beings. Only if that happens can women enter into public life retaining their capacity for care and nurture alongside their increased ability to take part in the public affairs of a country.

The power game leads to the breakdown of the family institution and, as side phenomena, to problems of divorce, problems with young people and children, problems in relation to the aged, the spread of alcoholism and, in general, loss of moral backbone among the people. As long as the women who break away from the established system of marital relations continue within the framework of the same general system, managing their households and taking care of their children as the heads of their own households, as is often the case both in rural and urban situations, they can somehow be accommodated. Solutions for problems which involve dealings with official authorities can be found on an *ad hoc* basis when they themselves are either incapable or, according to the social system, not permitted to appear on their own behalf. These kinds of arrangements will not work permanently. Women are not miracle-workers who can forever shoulder all the responsibility loaded onto them.

Prostitution is one of the outcomes of this situation. Another is an increased number of orphans, children whom the kin no longer claim. From time to time in the Tanzanian press the issue of 'dumping of babies' has arisen. The public is shocked by the news that newly-born babies are found dumped in conspicuous places. There is an uproar in the news media, and young women are blamed for their inhuman acts. There is also news of women poisoning their children or in some other way trying to get rid of them. In rural societies the pressures take the form of witchcraft and sorcery. Individual cases cannot always be excused in terms of the particular woman's social history; but as a general issue they are an outcome of the situation in which women are overwhelmed by desperation.

Looking back in history to the beginning of the women's road, the restrictions placed on them by their sanctioned roles as the bearers of offspring and carriers of believed life-energies were not a factor limiting either woman's value in society or her power. The unity of life within the realm of nature, of which the human being was only one constituent, assigned the woman the control over the life-generating and life-sustaining powers. The symbolic unity in which life's total substance was contained set the female element at its heart. The reproductive and productive forces were not to be separated from each other, and thus also the social relations based on them were not conceived apart from each other.

Before the market economy took over, the man did not 'own' the land while the woman tilled it. The man cleared the ground and broke it, the woman prepared it for cultivation, and together they sowed the seeds. The harvest belonged to them jointly but the woman had the control over its use. This had been the general pattern, which had its variations in local conditions, unless it was a question of non-cultivators, the herdsmen and women.

The people of the southern and eastern sectors of Tanzania honoured women as the root and stem of the family line, *ukoo* or *lukolo*. The women determined the leadership, and without them man had no place in society. It is difficult to fathom, with hindsight, the fundamental change in setting values that was gradually caused by the growth of trade, the influence of the exchange of goods and later the use of money.

However, it is not difficult to imagine how it was that the masculine freedom from the bodily restrictions of childbirth and nurture would lead the men to extend their adventures into the unclaimed zones beyond the domestic to adventurous contacts not only with untamed nature, through exploitation of its wildlife, but also with the utilisation of its mineral resources and exchange of goods.

The myths and histories of most ethnic groups tell that their leaders had their origins outside the original inhabitants. The precarious wealth which cattle meant for a population made it necessary for them to have a degree of mobility and thus also potential contact and conflict with other groups. It is natural that the herders, rather than the sedentary nurturers, were in a position to raid or trade in cattle and to become part of the ensuing quarrels over boundaries and territories. It was natural also in those circumstances that women, as the producers, fell prey to these quarrels and were the most strategic objects to be made use of in bargaining.

The domain of the domesticated and the domain of the outlying wild formed initially the basic division of responsibilities and roles between the sexes. It prepared the ground for similar division at the later stages in the society's development. Women had little share in public life and ultimately in determining the clan relations in terms of boundaries.

Yet it has been pointed out that women's personal abilities and talents enabled them in individual cases to become even rulers of extended territories, but it could be done usually only at the expense of their female roles. Whether as a chief or as a seeress or the keeper of a holy shrine, their becoming leaders coincided with the abolition or passing of their active regenerative role. Entering into public responsibilities created a conflict with the reproductive sphere of women's life.

It has been emphasized that the roles women played in the premonetary society did not have the potential to be converted to new modes in utilisation of power. They remained in the sphere of the numinous and the mythical. The power that women wielded was sufficient to sustain an internal balance of influence. It could be maintained as long as both sexes shared the same conceptualisation of the system of significant values.

The increasing influence of metropolitan capitalism affected the lives of both men and women, they were in the same position in relation to the often concealed forms of exploitation, which appeared in a garb of progress. But in this process men became the carriers of the external economic power into the local societies. The social systems became reshaped, and the value attached to land changed its nature, after the products of that land became the means of exchange instead of being principally a means of family maintenance.

As things evolved in Tanzanian societies, the woman's work in the domestic sphere was not given monetary value during the colonial time when the ethnic societies were united under the colonial government and their economy was linked up with the international monetary system. Women's work was embedded in the system as a concealed contribution to the colonial economy in supporting the underpaid wage labour by the maintenance of their families. Consequently, it lost its value in the eyes of men through whom its utilisation took place and who received monetary payment for their own part in labour. The studies from different parts of Tanzania in this book have described what has been the result of this development for the women and families.

As the result of the dislocation of the former balance of power, i.e. as the land became a means for producing crops for sale in monetary terms, so in the same way women became treated as a means of production (reproduction), producing both future labour power and marketable goods. Man became the manager and woman the worker. It was not necessary for the worker to have any right to the land she worked. She controlled only that part of the yield of the land which was needed for the maintenance of the home, but when the cash needs competed with the need for sustenance, the woman was pushed into a more and more difficult situation in which to manage the nurture of her family.

One of the basic facts brought out in this book is that the fundamental change in the situation of women took place through the new conception of land as a possession instead of as a means of common utilisation for common needs. When the product of land was given monetary value, the land itself was no longer conceived of as the given right of its user, a male or female member of the clan or lineage which utilised it. The separation of woman from her right to land separated her from a concrete means of wielding power. She became treated comparably to land and cattle, as a means of production (reproduction), and lost her own voice.

In those parts of the country where myth and ritual continue to form an important part of cultural life, the women still have creative, recognised roles, even if these roles are periodically suppressed and are actualised only on certain occasions. The roles have the potential of giving the woman self-esteem. It is no accident that self-confident women leaders have emerged from these societies despite the fact that their educational background has been weak.

The question remains as to how the women's strengths could find their rightful use in society. Some of the ways have been indicated. It has been suggested that if the villages are assisted in carrying out their plans in such a way that those members who do not have initial capital to invest in cooperative efforts, or do not have rights to inherited land, are also given the right to a plot of land, women will be in a situation to make full use of it and will not be left behind in any development thrust. It has also been pointed out that women do not need to be urged to take part in development: they are its mainstay. Whether they direct their efforts towards planned development or withdraw and utilise the informal sectors and informal channels for their own and their families' maintenance depends on how much of what I have called 'space' they manage to clear for their private and corporate lives within the given structures. In general, if the planned cooperative efforts within the village structure are directed for the benefit of those who really need them and are supported so that they become a success, it will also mean a great improvement in women's life. Women have been used to thinking in terms of working together with other women and men. They would continue to do this if the conditions were favourable and did not turn into a form of exploitation.

For present-day societies, not only in Tanzania but universally, the discovery of the processes through which women have been pushed to the margins of society should lead to the question of the ultimate values of human life and to a return to the sources. It has been pointed out that the failure to realise this leads women to use power in terms of monetary values just as men have already done for centuries. The breaking away of woman from the dominance of man is, for her part, an expression of her refusal to have her body used as a means for the production of wealth, in which she shares only marginally. Thus the question of the restoration to the woman of her rightful place in society also means a restoration of human values in the whole of society.

BIBLIOGRAPHY

Primary sources

Fieldnotes and personal collections of Marja-Liisa Swantz (MLS) and Lloyd Swantz (LS); Ministry of Information and Culture of Tanzania, Jipemoyo archives, abbreviated UTAF (= Utamaduni files), copies at the Institute of Development Studies, University of Helsinki.

Books and Articles

Anderson-Morshead, A.E.M., *The History of the Universities' Mission to Central Africa*, vol. I, *1859–1909*. Rev. edn, London, Universities' Mission to Central Africa, 1955.

Bachofen, J.J., *Das Mutterrecht*. Stuttgart, 1861.

Bader, Z.K., 'Women, Private Property and Production in Bukoba District'. Unpubl. M.A. thesis, University of Dar es Salaam, 1975.

Bailey, P.J.M., 'The Changing Economy of the Chagga Cultivator of Marangu, Kilimanjaro', *Geography*, 53, 1968.

Baur, R.P., *Voyage dans l'Oudoe et l'Ouzigoua* (Zanquebar) Lyon, Imp. Mougin-Rusand, 1882.

Beidelman, T., 'A history of Ukaguru 1851–1916', *Tanzania Notes and Records*, 1962, 58–9.

Boserup, E., *Women's Role in Economic Development*. London, Geo. Allen and Unwin, 1970.

Boulding, Elise, *Women, Peripheries and Food Production*. Mexico, International Peace Research Association General Conference, December 1977.

Brewin, D.R., 'Kilimanjaro agriculture', *Tanzania Notes and Records*, 64, 1965.

Bryceson, Deborah Fahy and Marjorie Mbilinyi, 'The changing role of Tanzanian women in production', *Jipemoyo 2*, ed. by A.O. Anacleti. Dept. of Research and Planning, Ministry of National Culture and Youth of Tanzania, and the Research Council for the Humanities, Academy of Finland, 1980.

Carlebach, J., *Juvenile Prostitute in Nairobi*. Kampala, East African Institute of Social Research, 1962.

Church Missionary Intelligence. 1882/8.

Claeson, C.-F. and B. Egero, *Migration and the Urban Population*. BRALUP Research Notes No. 11.2. University of Dar es Salaam, 1972. Also published in *Geografiska Annaler*, Ser. B., Stockholm, 1972.

Cory, Hans, and M.N. Hartnoll, *Customary Law of the Haya Tribe*. London, Lund Humphries, 1945.

Dundas, Charles, *Kilimanjaro and its People: a History of the Wachagga*. London, Frank Cass, 1968 (1st ed, 1924).

Egero, B., *Migration and Economic Development South of Lake Victoria*. BRALUP Research Paper 32, University of Dar es Salaam, 1974.

—— and Henin, R. (eds), *The Population of Tanzania: Census* Vol. 6. Dar es Salaam, BRALUP and Bureau of Statistics, 1973.

Engels, Frederick, *The Origin of the Family, Private Property and the State*, intro. Evelyn Read. New York, Pathfinder Press, 1976.

Epstein, A.L., 'Urbanization and Social Change in Africa', in Breeze, G. (ed.), *The City in Newly Developing Countries: Readings on Urbanism and Urbanization*. Englewood Cliffs, NJ, Prentice-Hall, 1972.

Feiermann, Steven, 'Documents in the History of the Kamba in Eastern Tanzania', paper presented to the seminar on the history of the East African Coast, Columbia University, 1974.

Freyhold, M.K., K. Sawaki and M. Zalla, Moshi District, in *The Young Child in Tanzania*. Dar es Salaam, National Scientific Research Council, UNICEF, 1973.

Gerber, W., *Lutherisches Missionsjahrbuch für das Jahr 1933*. Leipzig, Wallmann, n.d.

Godelier, M., *Perspectives in Marxist Anthropology*. Cambridge University Press, 1977.

Gustafsson, M., 'The position of the Haya women'. Mimeo. Uppsala, Church of Sweden Mission, 1972.

Gutmann, B., 'Problems of social organization in Africa', *Africa* (journal of International Inst. of African Languages and Cultures), I, 3, 1928, 511–15.

——, *Die Stammeslehren der Dschagga*, 3 vols. Munich, Beck, 1932–8.

Handbook of German East Africa. London, HMSO, 1916.

Henin, R. and B. Egero, *The 1967 Population Census of Tanzania: a demographic analysis*. BRALUP Research Paper no. 19, University of Dar es Salaam, 1972.

Himmelstrand, U. and F.O. Okediji, 'Social Structure and Motivational Tuning in Social and Economic Development', *Journal of Social Issues*, XXIV, 2, 1968, University of Ibadan, Nigeria.

Hydén, Göran, *Political Development in Rural Tanzania: TANU yajenga nchi*. Nairobi, East African Publishing House, 1969.

Iliffe, John, *Modern History of Tanganyika*. London, Cambridge University Press, 1979.

Johnston, Sir Harry Hamilton, *The Uganda Protectorate*. London, Hutchinson, 1902.

Jones, Thomas Jesse, *Education in East Africa*. London, Africa House Press, 1924.

Katoke, I.K., *The Karagwe Kingdom: A history of the Abanyambo of North-West Tanzania*. Nairobi, East African Publishing House, 1975.

——, *The Making of Karagwe Kingdom: Tanzania History from Oral Traditions*. Nairobi, East African Publishing House, 1970.

Kibira, J.M., 'A Study of Christianity among the Bahaya Tribe'. Unpubl. M.A. thesis, Boston University, 1964.

Kjekshus, Helge, *Ecology Control and Economic Development in East African History*. London, Heinemann, 1977.

Leslie, J.A.K., 'Some Aspects of African Life in Dar es Salaam'. Unpubl. typescript. Dar es Salaam, 1957.

Lindberg, O., Data on civil servants' wives' economic and occupational activities. Personal communication, 1974.

Little, Kenneth, *African Women in Towns*. Cambridge University Press, 1973.

MacRae, Phyllis, 'Elite Women in Tanzania: Patterns of Occupational Mobility'. Unpubl. M.A. thesis, University of Dar es Salaam, 1974.

Maro, P., 'Population and Land Resources in Northern Tanzania: the Dynamics of Change, 1920–1970'. Unpubl. Ph.D. thesis, University of Minnesota, 1974.

Mascarenhas, A.C. and J. Rudengren, 'Spatial Differentiation at Ward Level: the Case of Kahe, Kilimanjaro Region'. *East African Universities Social Science Conference*, Dar es Salaam, 1973.

Meinhof, Carl, *Afrikanische Rechtsgebräuche*. Berlin, Hamburgische Vorträge, Buchhandlung der Berliner Evangelische Missionsgesellschaft, 1914.

Moffett, J.P., *Handbook of Tanganyika*. 2nd edn. Dar es Salaam, Government Printer, 1958.

Moshi District Development Plan, 1974.

Nyerere, Julius K., *Freedom and Socialism: Uhuru na ujamaa*. Dar es Salaam, Oxford University Press, 1968.

Orodha ya watu wanaokabiliwa na Njaa Wilayani. Moshi, 1973/4.

Perkin, D.J., *Neighbours and Nationals in an African City Ward*. London, Routledge & Kegan Paul, 1969.

Philips, A., *Survey of African Marriage and Family Life*. Oxford University Press, 1953.

Redfield, R., *Peasant Society and Culture: an Anthropological Approach to Civilization*. Chicago, University of Chicago Press, 1956.

Rehse, H., *Kiziba. Land and People*. Stuttgart, Strecker and Schröder, 1910.

Reining, P.C., 'Haya Land Tenure: Landholding and Tenancy'. *Anthropological Quarterly*, 35, Apr. 1962, 58–73.

Reining, Priscilla, 'Social Factors and Food Production in an East African Peasant Society: the Haya', in S.M. Peter (ed.), *African Food Production Systems*. Baltimore, MacLoughlin, 1970.

Rudengren, J., *A Methodological Study of Population Density and Distribution: a Case Study of West Lake*. BRALUP Research Report 7, New Series, University of Dar es Salaam, 1974.

Sabot, R.H., *Education, Income Distribution, and Rates of Urban Migration in Tanzania*. ERB Paper no. 72.6, University of Dar es Salaam, 1972.

——, *Open Unemployment and the Employed Compound of Urban Surplus Labour*. ERB Paper no. 74.4, University of Dar es Salaam, 1974.

Sender, N., 'Farm Size and Population Pressure on Mt. Kilimanjaro'. Paper presented to East African Agricultural Society Conference, Dar es Salaam, April 1970.

Shanin, Teodor (ed.), *Peasants and Peasant Societies: Selected Readings*. Harmondsworth, Penguin, 1971.

Sicard, S. von, *The Lutheran Church on the Coast of Tanzania 1887–1914, with special reference to the Evangelical Lutheran Church in Tanzania, Synod of Uzaramo-Uluguru*. Lund, Gleerup, 1970.

Southall, A.W. and P.C.W. Gutkind, *Townsmen in the Making: Kampala and its Suburbs*. Kampala, East African Institute of Social Research, 1957.

Stahl, Kathleen, *History of the Chagga People of Kilimanjaro*. The Hague, Mouton, 1964.

Stuhlmann, F., Mit Emin Pascha ins Herz von Africa. Berlin, Dietrich Reimer, 1894.

Sundkler, B., *Ung kyrka i Tanganyika*. Uppsala, Church of Sweden Mission, 1947.

——, *Bara Bukoba*, Uppsala, Verbum, 1974; publ. in English as *Bara Bukoba: Church and Community in Tanzania*, London, C. Hurst, 1980.

Swantz, L.W. 'The Zaramo of Tanzania'. Unpubl. M.A. thesis, Syracuse University, 1965.

——, 'The Role of the Traditional Medicine Man in Dar es Salaam'. Unpubl. Ph.D. thesis, University of Dar es Salaam, 1977.

Swantz, Marja-Liisa, *Religious and Magical Rites of Bantu Women in Tanzania*. Dar es Salaam, 1966.

——, *Ritual and Symbol in Transitional Zaramo society*. Lund, Gleerup, 1970.

——, 'Ritual and Myth in Transitional Zaramo Society', *Temenos*, 8, 1972, 96–117.

——, *Research in Action as a Programme for University Students*. BRALUP Service Paper 73/7, University of Dar es Salaam, 1973.

——, *Youth and Development in the Coast Region of Tanzania*. BRALUP, NS 15, University of Dar es Salaam, 1973.

——, 'The Church and the Changing Role of Women in Tanzania'. Mimeo. Dar es Salaam, 1974.

——, 'Interaction of Islam and the African society on the East African coast', *Temenos*, 12, 1976, 136–48.

Tanganyika African National Union, *Katiba ya TANU*. Kampuni ya Taifa ya Uchapaji. Dar es Salaam, 1967.

——, *Mwelekeo wa Maendeleo ya Kijamaa Mkoani Kilimanjaro*. March 1974.

Tanzania, United Republic of, *1967 Census*, vols I–VI. Dar es Salaam, Bureau of Statistics.

——, *Tanzania Second Five-Year Plan for Economic and Social Development*, 1 July 1969–30 June 1974. Dar es Salaam, Government Printer, 1969.

Venermo, Kyösti, 'The Role of Spontaneous Housing in Up-country Towns of Tanzania, with special reference to Iringa'. Helsinki, unpubl. paper 1981.

Westergaard, M., 'Women and Work in Dar es Salaam'. Mimeo, Dept. of Sociology, University of Dar es Salaam, 1970.

Weule, Karl, *Native Life in East Africa*. New York, D. Appleton, 1909.

Wright, Marcia, 'Women in peril: a commentary on the life stories of captives in nineteenth-century East-Central Africa', *African Social Research*, 20, Dec. 1975, 800–19.

Young, Roland and Henry Fosbrooke, *Land and politics among the Luguru of Tanganyika*. London, Routledge & Kegan Paul, 1960.

Zalla, T.M., *Herd composition and farm management data on smallholder milk producers in Kilimanjaro: some preliminary results*. Research Bureau Paper 74.8, University of Dar es Salaam, 1974.

Akesson, Birgit, *Källvattnets mask, Om dans i Afrika*, Stockholm, Atlantis, 1983

INDEX